TIMES OF GREATNESS

MORALITY MATTERS

by
GEORGE E PFAUTSCH

authorHOUSE™

1663 LIBERTY DRIVE, SUITE 200
BLOOMINGTON, INDIANA 47403
(800) 839-8640
WWW.AUTHORHOUSE.COM

First published by AuthorHouse 08/12/05

ISBN: 1-4208-7189-7 (sc)

Library of Congress Control Number: 2005906784

Printed in the United States of America
Bloomington, Indiana

This book is printed on acid-free paper.

<u>ACKNOWLEDGEMENTS AND</u>
<u>THANKS</u>

The verification of certain historical information for this book was obtained from data maintained by several federal government Web sites; primarily the United States Information Agency and the White House. Visits to a number of presidential museums and libraries were useful in providing additional insights to many of our country's leaders.

Thanks to my wife, Dodi, for her patience during the hours I spent in front of my computer and to Mary Lu for her editing and technical assistance.

Contents

INTRODUCTION

Throughout the history of civilization, many empires and nations have had the label of *great.* In most cases, the label "great" has been synonymous with "powerful." But have most powerful empires and nations really been great nations? Many powerful nations achieved their might through military conquests. The demise of many of those nations was often at the hands of other conquerors.

In ancient history, the ruling empires of Egypt, Assyria, Babylon, and Greece achieved power through the strength of their armies, but the armies, over the long run, did not prevail. The concern for their citizens varied, but these empires were not necessarily greatly concerned with the welfare of their people. The quest for power was a driving force. Freedom for the people within parts of these empires was frequently not a major consideration.

The Roman Empire also achieved power through conquests, and ruled their empires with an iron hand. That empire decayed from within.

When moving to modern times, the beginning of the twentieth century opened with strong empires in Russia, France, England, Germany, and Austria/Hungary. Some are still strong nations, but probably have less relative strength today than they had a hundred years ago. The diminishment of their relative strength has been due to the superpower status of the United States.

Were all of the aforementioned great nations? That depends on one's definition. If power alone determines greatness, then all of the nations and empires previously mentioned achieved that status. However, those nations did not necessarily achieve greatness because of their great concern for their own citizens or humanity in general. Without a deep and sincere concern for the citizens of its country, a nation does not deserve the label of "great."

No nation has had as great a beginning as the United States. It declared its independence because the founding fathers believed that a new nation deserved to exist, in order to give citizens the unalienable rights of life, liberty, and pursuit of happiness, which were endowed by a Creator. Despite human rights violations to blacks and other minorities at various times, this country demonstrated a high regard for humanity throughout most of its existence. Through the combination of achieving power while maintaining a high regard for our Creator, and for its citizens and universal humanity, the United States deserves the title of one of the greatest, if not the greatest nation, that has ever existed. The founding fathers were an exceptional group of people, who were ingenious in their establishment of this country. With the Constitution, they created an outstanding document to guide the nation.

Our Constitution has survived more than 215 years. For most of its existence, it has guided this nation in the enactment of new laws. Until recent years, the citizens of this country had a great appreciation and understanding of the greatness of the Constitution. They also understood that our founding fathers declared independence and wrote a constitution that had faith-based morality as an underpinning. They did not subscribe to either a religion-based or a secular-based morality to provide the proper code of conduct for a nation, which would welcome immigrants with diverse religious and ethnic backgrounds.

A faith-based morality is simply based on a broad belief of a supernatural Creator, that such a belief encompasses the understanding of his greatness, and that the people he created treat each other with love and kindness. In order for any nation to truly deserve the label of "great," it must govern according to the standards of faith-based morality. Within a country that believes in a Supreme Creator, the Ten Commandments (with some variation thereof by Muslims), are the most common guidelines for the code of proper conduct in a faith-based morality. Religion-based morality carries the code of conduct into a much more detailed and broader definition of morality, whereas a secular-based morality lacks any underpinning for a proper code of conduct. Secular-based morality is more apt to change as the culture of a country changes.

In most aspects, this country adhered to a faith-based morality throughout most of its existence. However, in recent years, it has begun moving toward a secular morality, which threatens the greatness of this country. In my previous book, *Redefining Morality,* I reviewed the threats to our nation of turning toward a secular-based morality.

It is interesting to speculate how long the United States can maintain its status of a great nation. In order to maintain that status, it is the contention of this author that this country must continue to base its laws on a faith-based morality, as intended by our founding fathers. That type of morality resulted in the Constitution and laws which are intended to achieve a high level of general welfare of its own citizens, while also maintaining a high regard for the human rights of individual citizens within its own country, as well as the rest of the world. That type of morality must also be grounded in the belief of a supernatural Creator, and that such a Creator has a better sense of moral righteousness than that possessed by humans.

There is an interesting quotation in a book attributed to a Scottish professor, which was supposedly written in the middle of the eighteenth century. There is some question as to the validity of the quotation as well as the book, but it is of some interest in assessing the duration of governments.

The alleged quotation is attributed to a Professor Alexander Tyler (a Professor Tytler did exist at about that time), and was made in regards to the Athenian Republic. It goes as follows:

> *"A democracy cannot exist as a permanent form of government. It can only exist until the voters discover that they can vote themselves money from the public treasury. From that moment on, the majority always votes for the candidates promising the most money from the public treasury, with the result that a democracy always collapses over loose fiscal policy followed by a dictator. The average age of the world's great civilizations has been two hundred years. These nations have progressed through the following sequence: from bondage to spiritual faith, from spiritual faith to great courage, from courage to liberty, from liberty to abundance, from abundance to selfishness, from selfishness to complacency, from complacency to apathy, from apathy to dependency, from dependency back to bondage."*

That supposed quotation does not deal directly with morality, but it does give insights as to what can happen to people and governments over extended periods.

Even if the quotation is fictional, it provides an interesting insight regarding the rise and decline of nations. To the extent that it helps support opinions regarding the rise and possible beginning decline of the United States, we will make occasional references to the quotation.

There is no doubt that the United States has progressed to a nation of abundance, and there is some evidence that we are a more selfish group of citizens than were our forefathers. One can also argue that we have become a more complacent, apathetic, and dependent society. When such complacency and apathy extends to faith-based morality, a nation is in trouble.

There is also considerable evidence that selfishness tends to cause citizens to favor socialism once they taste some dose of it, even if ever-increasing taxes are ultimately necessary to pay for the government's supposed largesse. The thought of getting something in the short-term from the government, even if the cost in the long-term is higher, does have an attraction to people. Politicians are very adept at exploiting that weakness in people. It also gives the politicians a greater amount of power, as they have a greater voice in the redistribution of wealth. It often does not matter to them that all citizens may be poorer in the long-term.

There is no doubt that this country has had periods, especially during recessions and depressions, when small doses of socialism were appropriate. The problem is that it is almost impossible to remove social programs, even if they have become unnecessary. Is government to blame? Yes, to some degree, but all citizens share the blame. As the alleged quote of Professor Tyler states, voters do tend to vote for those who promise the most. That is true, even if the government programs that are promised could be run more efficiently by the private sector, or were non-existent.

From the discovery of this country in 1492 until the present time, this land of ours has undergone periods of greatness, and periods of trials and tribulation. In this book, we will examine the entire history of this nation and explore those periods when we were a great country, and also those periods when greatness was lacking. The measurement of greatness will be those periods when government did most for humanity, especially the citizens of this country, while maintaining laws grounded in a faith-based morality, which always accrue to the general welfare of all.

CHAPTER 1 --- COLUMBUS TO REVOLUTION

Prior to the discovery of this country in 1492, the Western Hemisphere was home to millions of people, who would eventually be labeled "Indians" by Christopher Columbus. Although, some tribes of Indians, such as the Aztecs and Incas, developed cultures that were quite advanced, these people lived in isolation from the rest of the world continents. They were not known to people of other continents and were unaware of the existence of other people or continents.

That isolation changed in 1492, when Christopher Columbus discovered what became known as the "Americas." On October 12, 1492, while on a voyage for Spain, Columbus accidentally discovered the New

World. The purpose of his exploration was to search for a direct sea route to the Far East. When he discovered land in the Caribbean, he believed he had found the land Marco Polo reached in his overland travels to China. Because he believed he had reached "the Indies," he named the people "Indians." From that point in history, the isolation of Native Americans was over.

From the time of the discovery of the New World, the culture and mores of Native Americans began giving way to the culture and mores of the Europeans, who began coming to this "new" country.

The first Europeans who came to America were the explorers. Cortez came and defeated the Aztecs, and conquered Mexico. Other explorers from several countries of Europe included De Leon, Coronado, De Soto, Cartier, Cabot, Champlain, Hudson, and many others. With them came the beginnings of new cultures. Some came, explored, and returned, while others came and died here. All began contributing to a new and different culture in the region they explored.

The first Europeans to settle in the New World came to the Spanish colonies in Mexico, the West Indies, and South America. To this day, these colonies have maintained the Spanish language, and the Spanish influence is notable in many aspects of those regions.

In the early seventeenth century, two English colonies were established in this country, which would have an impact on this country to the present day. The colonies, in Jamestown, Virginia and Plymouth, Massachusetts, brought with them the grassroots of a culture that would affect not only our culture, but also the establishment of a government. These colonies were established in regions, which would give the country its first six presidents.

They were regions that would also provide many of the early statesmen of the country. These statesmen had a significant role in the Declaration of Independence and the establishment of the new nation's Constitution.

These two colonies would also have another significant impact on the morality of the country. Slavery was introduced in the early stages of the Virginia colony, whereas it was never introduced in the Massachusetts colony. The issue of slavery would be a blemish on this country until the Civil War was fought, during which more Americans were killed on our native soil than any other war in which this country has been engaged.

Some of the early English settlers came to this country for the adventure and opportunities that were not to be found in their homeland. However, most came to escape political oppression, and to seek a place where they were free to practice their religion. Between 1620 and 1635, England underwent a long economic recession. Freedom and economic opportunities were highly motivating to those who dared take the journey to a land with which they were not familiar.

The early English immigrants were welcomed to a land of dense forests that ran along most of the East Coast. These forests provided game, firewood, and the materials needed to build houses and furniture. Friendly Indians taught them to grow many of the vegetables that sustained the early settlers.

English settlers continued to migrate to the New World during the arbitrary reign of Charles I in the 1630's. After Cromwell defeated the allies of Charles I, many more Englishmen who were on the wrong side of the struggle, fled to this country. Immigrants from the German-speaking regions of Europe also fled to this new country to escape political and religion oppression fostered upon them by the ruling princes of those regions.

The other colonies were developed in a variety of ways. William Penn, a Quaker, was instrumental in the development of the Pennsylvania colony. Penn's religious background resulted in a colony that was very conscious of religious freedom and tolerance, and had a sincere concern for the equality of its citizens. In Georgia, many of the early immigrants were convicts who were permitted to migrate to this country instead of serving prison terms.

Many of the early settlers could not afford the costs involved with crossing the Atlantic to live in this new country. In numerous cases, the shipping companies, the captains of ships, and agents from companies such as the Virginia or Massachusetts Bay Companies, would pay the passage costs in return for the "indentured servants" agreeing to work as contract laborers for periods of four-to-seven years.

Did the early years of colonization of the country suggest future greatness? The answer has some elements of yes, and some of no. The courage and risk-taking required to immigrate to an unknown land, in search of freedom and liberty not otherwise obtainable, gave this nation a core of citizens who would endure many dangers to obtain the unalienable rights subsequently addressed in the Declaration of Independence. These early settlers were the first in a long line of determined and strong-willed people who placed a high value on freedom.

On the other side of the scale, not all humans were permitted to share in the early quests for freedom. Native Americans suffered and died in their struggle to maintain the land they long roamed without interference. Slavery also got its start in the seventeenth century, and would continue for a period of 200 years.

By 1690, the population of the colonies had increased to 250,000. In addition to immigrants from England and Germany, the population included people from the Dutch countries and Sweden, as well as a few from France, Spain, Italy, Portugal, and several other European countries.

The colonies developed rapidly through the period of the early eighteenth century, and by the middle of the eighteenth century the population of the colonies had increased to 1.5 million.

In 1754, a threat by France endangered British interests in the colonies and the colonies themselves. In the struggle known as the French and Indian Wars, England ultimately prevailed. In the Peace of Paris Treaty, signed in 1763, France relinquished all of Canada, the Great Lakes, and the upper Mississippi Valley to England.

The threat to the colonies from France was overcome with the Peace of Paris Treaty, but a new problem soon developed for the colonies. England recognized that its vast new empire in North America was going to require greater governance. In turn, greater governance for defense and administration was going to require new sources of revenue.

In attempting to achieve larger revenues from the colonies, the British parliament passed several measures, including the Sugar and Stamp Acts. These acts, which were a form of taxation on the colonies, also were accompanied by stronger central control and the resulting diminishment of colonial self-government. From these acts came the colonial slogan of "taxation without representation."

With pressure from the colonies and British merchants, who were being economically harmed by colonial boycotts, the British government, in 1766, repealed the Stamp Act and modified the Sugar Act. However, in order to appease the supporters of central control, the Parliament also passed the Declaratory Act. This act gave Parliament the authority to make laws binding the colonies "in all cases whatsoever."

A series of other incidents, such as the Townsend Acts (which imposed more duties), continued to create tensions between the colonists and the British government. The "Boston Massacre" in 1770 gave impetus to the early urgings for independence. Only five people were killed by British soldiers in the incident that became known as a massacre. To some degree, the massacre was instigated by the colonists. Nevertheless, it increased the clamoring for independence.

On December 16, 1773, the "Boston Tea Party" occurred. Colonists, led by Samuel Adams, and who were disguised as Mohawk Indians, boarded three British ships and dumped their tea cargo into Boston Harbor. This was done to ensure that the foreign tea would not be sold in the colonies.

The Boston Tea Party was followed by a series of new laws imposed on the colonies, which were called the "Coercive or Intolerable Acts." On September 5, 1774, delegates from all thirteen colonies (except Georgia) assembled in Philadelphia to review the acts they considered to be oppressive, and to induce the British government to make concessions. This gathering of the "First Continental Congress" passed a series of resolutions, including the rights of colonists to life, liberty, and property. The Congress also formed the "Continental Association," which among other things, provided for retaliatory measures against the British Acts. Pro-independence leaders, who began urging revolution and independence, led the association. They also were responsible for collecting military supplies and mobilizing troops.

More moderate leaders in the colonies urged discussions with the British government for compromise. King George III of England, in turn, demanded submission.

On April 19, 1775, the beginning of events occurred which were the final steps to revolution and independence. A British general, Thomas Gage, sent a group of his troops to Concord to confiscate munitions being stockpiled by colonists. On reaching Lexington, the British troops encountered a group of seventy "Minutemen." In the encounter, eight were left dead and several were wounded. The encounter became referred to as "the shot heard around the world."

After the Lexington encounter, the British troops continued on to Concord and destroyed what amount of munitions remained after much had been removed by the colonists. The British march from Lexington to Concord, and then back to Boston, gave the colonial militia time to mobilize, and more than 250 British soldiers were killed before the remainder returned to Boston.

With the events of Lexington and Concord still fresh in their minds, the colonial leaders gathered in

Philadelphia on May 10, 1775. At this gathering, the "Second Continental Congress" was convened. By May 15, the Congress voted to go to war against England. Colonel George Washington was appointed commander in chief of the American forces. Not all colonial leaders were in favor of war, but attempted agreements with England failed. In August 1775, King George III proclaimed the colonies to be in rebellion.

A great nation was about to be born. From 1492 through the end of 1775, the major indication of greatness was the intense desire possessed by the colonists for freedom, and the fearlessness displayed by explorers and settlers in the development of a new and strange land. Most of them also possessed a deep faith in their Creator. At the end of 1775, the land that was to become the United States had a collection of leaders who were about to pave the way that would lead to the greatest nation ever known to mankind.

CHAPTER 2 --- A GREAT BEGINNING

One year after the Second Continental Congress first met, a resolution was passed which called for the colonies to become separated from England. Shortly thereafter, another resolution was passed, which declared that the colonies should be free and independent states. A committee of five, headed by Thomas Jefferson, was then appointed to draft a formal declaration of independence.

In early 1776, a relatively new immigrant to the colonies, Thomas Paine, published a small book called *Common Sense*. In that pamphlet, he stated his belief that two alternatives existed for the colonies: one was to continue to be submissive to King George III, whom he believed would continue to be a tyrannical ruler; the second alternative was to become an independent nation. *Common Sense* was written in January 1776, and within three months, 100,000 copies of the book were sold. The book gave considerable impetus to those who were ultimately responsible for voting for independence.

Jefferson spent considerable time during the month of June 1776, drafting the Declaration of Independence. It is not totally clear if the declaration drafted by Jefferson was primarily based on his own beliefs and thoughts or if he attempted to divorce himself from his own thoughts and incorporated the input of others, especially those on the committee. In any event, it is one of the nation's most cherished documents. The declaration did include the ideals that had been expressed by many colonial leaders and philosophers, especially John Locke. He, maybe more than anyone else, expressed his strong belief in the universal natural rights of every human being. Whether intended or not, Jefferson expressed in the declaration the basic elements of a faith-based morality which were to guide this nation.

A portion of the Declaration of Independence follows:

"When in the course of human events, it becomes necessary for one people to dissolve the political bands which have connected them with another, and to assume among the powers of the earth, the separate and equal station, to which the Laws of

Nature and <u>NATURE'S GOD</u> entitle them, a decent respect to the opinions of mankind requires that they should declare the causes which impel them to the separation."

"We hold these truths to be self-evident, that all men are created equal, that they are <u>ENDOWED BY THEIR CREATOR</u> with certain unalienable Rights, that among these are Life, Liberty, and the pursuit of Happiness."

(Emphasis and underlining added)

No greater document has ever been created for reasons to establish a nation, and for which a nation should exist. On July 4, 1776, the declaration was formally approved, and a new nation came into existence.

The war effort being led by General Washington was ebbing back and forth, and the war continued for a number of years. In October 1781, the surrender of Cornwallis at Yorktown brought a reduction in hostilities.

Although some battles continued, a new British government decided to pursue peace negotiations. The negotiations began in Paris in early 1782. In April 1783, Congress approved a final treaty. The treaty recognized the independence of the thirteen colonies, which then became states. To the new nation, Great Britain granted the territory west to the Mississippi, north to Canada and south to Florida, which was returned to Spain.

Five years elapsed after the Paris Peace Treaty was signed before a group of state representatives gathered in May 1787. The Federal Convention that gathered at the Philadelphia State House elected George Washington as its presiding officer. Washington, at that point, was regarded as the country's outstanding citizen, not only for his military leadership, but also for his integrity.

Although the convention had been assembled to draft amendments to the Articles of Confederation, it did not take long to proceed with building an entirely new form of government. Throughout the summer, the members of the convention labored to complete a draft, which organized the most complex government ever formed. On September 17, 1787, the Constitution was signed.

As was true of the Declaration of Independence, the Constitution was, and is, a masterpiece on providing the best guidelines for the governance of a nation. It has now served this nation for more than 215 years.

This nation was off to a great beginning, not perfect, but great. What were the ingredients of greatness? In the Declaration of Independence, recognition was made to the entitlement of people for certain powers from the Laws of Nature and Nature's God. It also recognized that the unalienable rights of life, liberty, and the pursuit of happiness were endowed by a Creator. No differentiation was made between Nature's God and the Creator. These words of the declaration essentially stated that the morality of a country should be predicated on a faith-based morality. Such a morality gave recognition to the existence of a God, that he created people with certain extraordinary rights, and when government did not properly provide those rights, then the people deserved to form a new government. WITHOUT THOSE RECOGNITIONS, A DECLARATION OF INDEPENDENCE, A NEW COUNTRY, AND A NEW CONSTITUTION FOR THE NEW COUNTRY WOULD NOT HAVE BEEN NECESSARY.

We have been fortunate to have had some great leaders, who understood that the civil rights of human beings must flow from a faith-based morality. Despite the opinion of the Supreme Court in the *Dred Scott v. Sanford* case, Abraham Lincoln understood that African Americans had a moral right to equality, even if the Supreme Court did not find that right in the Constitution. Martin Luther King also understood the moral right of civil disobedience when civil laws were not grounded in a faith-based morality.

Eleven years after the declaration was signed, the Constitution stated that the country would not be bound by any specific religion-based morality, nor could a logical person read the two documents together and believe there was any intent for the country to be bound by a secular-based morality. The founding fathers understood (better than our current government leaders) that tyranny could exist under a specific religion-based morality, or under a secular-based morality. The declaration and the Constitution have to this date precluded the tyrannies that tend to exist or come into existence when a country bases its laws and national code of conduct on religion or secular morality.

When government separates itself from religion, and religion separates itself from government, both are permitted to operate in their best and purest form. It would serve the general welfare of this country if people of faith, people of religions, and people of government remembered that at all times. Faith-based morality in government also permits those who do not wish to belong to any religion to enjoy that right and freedom within such a country. Faith, as well as denial of faith, is a powerful human motivator. The suppression of religion rarely works and the involvement of government in religion rarely works. History has proven, again and again, that nations with state religions become intolerant of those who do not belong to the state religion, and history has also proven that secular morality can be even worse.

Faith-based morality, as a standard for the conduct of government and a nation, may not be perfect, but it has been as close as humans may ever get to perfection. The founding fathers gave recognition to a supernatural power, "Nature's God" and the "Creator," who endowed all people with certain unalienable rights. In the First Amendment of the Constitution, it permitted all men to honor, or not honor, their vision of God by the words "Congress shall make no law respecting an establishment of religion, or prohibiting the free exercise thereof." However, the First Amendment DID NOT, AND DOES NOT, RESTRICT FAITH BEING EXPRESSED THROUGH SYMBOLS INDICATING SUCH FAITH. Today our judicial system seems to have considerable difficulty distinguishing religion from faith.

But, within the constitution created by our founding fathers, other considerations were also made that were the ingredients of greatness. Three branches of federal government were created, but the powers of the executive, legislative, and judicial arms were so well balanced that none could gain control.

Considerable more debate took place on the matter of representation in the legislative branch. To some degree, we are fortunate that the original thirteen states were comprised of large and small states. In what was a long and arduous debate, it was finally concluded that one house would be represented according to population, while the other house of Congress would have equal numbers from each state. The three branches of government were initially given broad powers, but the needs of future generations of the country were also considered by giving the legislative branch the future right to pass all necessary and proper laws. Despite their frequent attempts to gain such power, it does not belong to the judicial branch of government.

On the other hand, the founding fathers also wanted to prevent the Constitution from frequent and possibly unnecessary changes by requiring, in Article V, that "The Congress, whenever two-thirds of both Houses shall deem it necessary, shall propose Amendments to this Constitution, or, on the Application of the Legislatures of two-thirds of the several States, shall call a Convention for proposing Amendments---." A magnificent document was not to be changed easily.

On December 15, 1791, the first ten amendments, known as the Bill of Rights were ratified. In 1795, Amendment XI was passed, and in 1805, Amendment XII was passed, which established the method to be used in electing the president and the vice president.

It is a tribute to our founding fathers that from 1805 until the present time, only fifteen additional amendments have been added to the Constitution.

Not only was the new nation blessed with an outstanding constitution, but it also was blessed with great leadership. George Washington became our first president on April 30, 1789. He was not a highly educated individual, and began his working life as a surveyor while still a teenage youth. Thereafter, most of his adult life (until the Revolutionary War), was spent in the military, or overseeing his plantation in Mount Vernon. During the Revolutionary War, he served as commander in chief of the colonial forces. Washington was a man of great leadership skills, both as commander in chief and as our nation's first president. He often stayed above the partisan battles between his subordinates and let Congress do their job. He was the right man at the right time, and was respected by his peers and the citizens.

Following Washington as president was John Adams, who had served eight years as vice president under Washington. He was very unlike Washington in stature and personality, but, was also a man who sacrificed much of his personal life to serve in numerous governmental capacities, at home and abroad. Whereas Washington was a tall and somewhat quiet man, Adams was short, combative, and somewhat stubborn, but a true patriot.

Adams, as opposed to Washington, was well educated at Harvard. His early adult years were spent as teacher and lawyer. He served his nation in many roles. He was a delegate to the First and Second Continental Congresses, and was a strong advocate for independence. Later, he served in diplomatic roles in France and Holland. During his tenure in France, he was instrumental in negotiating the Paris Peace Treaty. From 1785 to 1788, he was the minister to the Court of St. James in England. After eight years as vice president under Washington, and another four years as president, he returned to his farm in Quincy, Massachusetts in 1801, and remained there until his death. Adams accomplished much for this nation and has been one of its most underrated presidents. His stubborn adherence to his principles did not always endear him to his peers and thus limited his political skills.

On July 4, 1826, John Adams, the advocate of independence, passed away. On the same date, the man who drafted the declaration, Thomas Jefferson, also died. In their twilight years, these two men exchanged hundreds of letters.

The eighteenth century came to a close as our national capitol was moved to its permanent home in Washington, D.C. A great nation was in its state of infancy, and had been served by two outstanding presidents, who were both instrumental in obtaining freedom and liberty for their citizens.

As the eighteenth century ended, our country was a great nation, even though it was not a powerful nation at that point. It was a nation founded on a faith-based morality, which meant that its national morality would be predicated on the belief in the goodness of a supernatural power (the "God of Nature and the Creator"). It was also great because it believed in the equality of all people and that those people had the unalienable right to life, liberty, and the pursuit of happiness. A nation was created with a constitution that stipulated the rights of citizens in the first ten amendments. Those were important to all citizens even if individuals and groups abuse those rights.

It was a great nation, but not perfect. Slavery existed, women were denied the right to vote, and the treatment of Native Americans did not imply equality for them. When a nation does not treat all citizens with the rights that assume they are equal in the eyes of a Creator, and a Creator endowed such rights, it lacks adherence to the standards of a faith-based morality. Our nation was a great country in 1800, but not perfect. It also was not a perfect nation in 2000, and its flaws in 2000 were as bad (or worse) than they were in 1800.

In 1800, it certainly had a better understanding of the morality that is most needed for a nation to observe the best standards of conduct.

CHAPTER 3 --- THE EARLY NINETEENTH CENTURY

Thomas Jefferson was the third president of our country, and the first to be elected in the nineteenth century. Jefferson was a complex individual, but this country will be forever indebted to the man who made substantial contributions to its early existence.

Jefferson was born in 1743 to a wealthy family, and was well educated at the College of William and Mary. Jefferson became involved in political life at the age of twenty-five. He served as a member of the Continental Congress, and was one of the five members on the committee to draft the Declaration of Independence. He was the sole writer of the first draft of the declaration.

Jefferson held many offices in his distinguished career. He was a minister to France, and due to his duties there, played no role in the ratification of the Constitution. He was secretary of state under Washington and served as vice president under Adams, before being elected president. His major achievement as president was the Louisiana Purchase.

It is somewhat ironic that the drafter of the declaration, in which the God of Nature and the Creator were given recognition, may also have been one of the least religious of our presidents. He was proof that a faith-based moralist need not be a religion-based moralist in order to be a great leader or a great man. Jefferson had no problem whatsoever with the concept of faith-based morality, but was clear in his writings that he would not have endorsed a religion-based morality.

Jefferson's two predecessors to the nation's highest office were also not highly religious men, although Washington did order that chaplains should be part of the military, and that men in the military should have the opportunity to worship. Washington, Adams, and Jefferson were deists, and through their words and actions, indicated their belief in the rights of all men to be free. However, the greatness of this nation at that time was also attributable to its citizens, to whom the freedoms ensured by the founding fathers were of utmost importance, and for which they came to this country and for which they would fight and die. However, the greatness of the country was flawed by the existence of slavery, the absence of the right to vote for women, and the treatment of Native Americans.

James Madison followed Jefferson to the presidency in 1809. During his two terms in office, this nation fought the War of 1812, which gave the United States a higher standing among other nations of the world, even though the war's results were somewhat inconclusive. In his early adult years, Madison played a significant role in the drafting of the Constitution, and in obtaining the first ten amendments, the Bill of Rights.

After Madison, James Monroe became the fifth president of the country. His address to Congress, which became known as the Monroe Doctrine, warned European powers against intervening in the affairs of the Western Hemisphere. During his administration, the Missouri Compromise also occurred, which admitted Missouri to the nation as a slave state and Maine as a free state. Many in the northern states of the country had hoped that slavery would slowly disappear, but the Missouri Compromise indicated that slavery had become such a part of plantations in the southern states that eliminating it would create a serious issue to all the nation. Despite the words "self-evident truths" and "unalienable rights" in the Constitution, the slaves were denied such rights.

John Quincy Adams, son of the second president, became the sixth president in 1825. He had a long and distinguished career to his country. At the age of twenty-six, he was appointed the minister to the Netherlands, and subsequently served in Germany and Russia. He was also a senator, and was a distinguished secretary of state under James Monroe.

In addition to the founding fathers and the early presidents, there was another man who made a strong imprint on the future governance of this country. In 1801, John Marshall became the chief justice of the Supreme Court, and held that office until 1835. Marshall was a strong defender of the Constitution. Many cases were heard during his office that involved constitutional issues. His most important legacy may have been his clarity regarding the rights of the Supreme Court to review and determine the constitutionality of laws passed by the Congress or by state legislatures. That may have been his greatest imprint on this country, but it also put an inordinate amount of power in the judicial branch of government. During his term, he clearly established that the Court would at least be a co-equal partner to Congress and the president in the governance of the country.

In the early nineteenth century, the westward flow of people accelerated, and as people moved west, many new states were added to the Union. The people were a hearty mixture of all types and found a freedom to reach their goals. Of necessity, they were a combination of farmer and hunter. They grew their own grain, vegetables, and fruit, raised their own livestock, and hunted for many of their meals. Some bought small parcels of land, and frequently speculators bought large parcels of land. Doctors, lawyers, businessmen, and others followed, but the farmer was the backbone of the newly populated lands. They were a hardworking group of people who for very small sums could obtain considerable amount of land. Most of the migration in the early nineteenth century went no further west than Missouri.

In 1829, the hero of the Battle of New Orleans became our seventh president. Andrew Jackson was the first president who did not call Massachusetts or Virginia home. He was born in the Carolinas and later moved to Tennessee. He was a flamboyant and feisty man. He was very much involved in the Indian wars, which drove many of the Cherokee and others westward, especially to Oklahoma. He was a popular man among the people who had moved westward and was the first president elected by most of the population.

Jackson was followed by a number of one-term presidents. His loyal supporter, Martin Van Buren, became the eighth president in 1837. William Henry Harrison became the ninth president, in 1841, but served only a month before he succumbed to pneumonia. He was our first president to die in office. His vice president, John Tyler, served until 1845. Following Tyler to the presidency was our eleventh president, James Polk, and in 1849, Zachary Taylor succeeded him. In 1850, Taylor became our second president to die in office.

By 1850, the population of this country had grown to more than twenty million. Land was very inexpensive to obtain, and the opportunity to prosper was available to many of the new immigrants from Europe. They enjoyed a freedom not available to most of them before coming to this country. With the Louisiana Purchase and the acquisition of Florida from Spain, the United States was shaped west to the Mississippi River in the manner that we know today. Most of the states east of the Mississippi had become a part of the United States by the middle of the nineteenth century.

In that same period of time, and following the famous battle at the Alamo, Texas, too, became a state, and expansion into area west of the Mississippi began. This country was thriving, and freedom was a precious part of many immigrants' new lives. However, some other situations remained that detracted from the greatness and goodness of this country.

We have already noted the treatment of the eastern Native American tribes, especially the Cherokee, who were forced to migrate to Oklahoma. It is somewhat unfair to judge other generations, because the culture of the times was so different. It is difficult to understand how we might be treated if people from another planet were to invade, conquer, and occupy our country at this time. We can only hope that we would be treated better than our forefathers treated many of the Native Americans.

Even if the treatment of the Native Americans could be somewhat rationalized, but not justified, the treatment of slaves could not. Despite the precious understanding of freedom our forefathers extended to European immigrants, the slaves were treated as less than human beings. Anytime one group of humans treats another group of humans as less than human, it violates the very essence of faith-based morality. It also violated the concept of humans expressed in the Declaration of Independence and the Constitution. Nothing can justify the shameful treatment of the slaves.

Slavery was, and forever will be, a disgrace to our country. It was a system of brutality. It was frequently accompanied by floggings, and slaves were often sold away from the surroundings of their own family. Slavery simply ignored the unalienable right of life, liberty, and the pursuit of happiness.

It is difficult to put the label of greatness on a country, which after existing for more than fifty years, treated slaves (as well as Native Americans) so inhumanely. It violated the basic concept of faith-based morality, which requires that all humans treat each other as they wish to be treated. It is not only difficult to put the label of greatness on such a country, and because of slavery and the treatment of Native Americans, we will refrain from putting that label on this country at the mid-point of the nineteenth century. It was a great opportunity for many European immigrants, but that alone cannot be enough to justify the national morality of that period. Slavery had been an issue in the political arena of this country, but abolition was delayed too long.

A nation, which was founded on the belief of the self-evident truth that all men are created equal, could not much longer accept the blight of slavery on its national conscience. The country was fortunate to have in place a constitution that had the right words, but was unfortunate in the lack of application of those words to all human beings who lived in this country.

CHAPTER 4---SLAVERY AND ABRAHAM LINCOLN

During the early part of the nineteenth century, slavery became a political and sectional issue in this country. By the middle of the nineteenth century, somewhere between 40,000 and 50,000 plantations throughout the southern states each owned at least twenty slaves, and more than half of the slaves worked on such plantations. The owners of these plantations were powerful in a political sense and had a major economic interest in maintaining slavery.

Although some of the smaller farmers of the south also owned slaves, many did not. Nevertheless, many of the poorer whites of the south also favored slavery, because they feared that if the slaves were free, they would compete for jobs and land. In that environment, many of the people, including businessmen, professional people, and political leaders, also supported the maintenance of slavery.

Abolitionists in the northern states became more and more adamant in a free-soil movement for any additional states coming into the Union and in their opposition to the entire idea of slavery. It soon became a national political issue.

Texas, which entered the Union in the 1840's, permitted slavery. The areas of California, New Mexico, and Utah did not have slavery. As the United States prepared to take over these territories in the late 1840's, southerners insisted that they be open to slaveholders, whereas the opposite viewpoint prevailed among northern states.

In 1850, Vice President Millard Fillmore became the thirteenth president of the country, following the death of Zachary Taylor. Fillmore was a supporter of the Compromise of 1850, which had been crafted by Henry Clay. The compromise was a series of resolutions regarding the issue of slavery, which temporarily kept the nation united. In future years, Fillmore would oppose many of the policies of Abraham Lincoln during the Civil War.

In 1853, Franklin Pierce became our fourteenth president. After the Compromise of 1850, it was assumed that the nation would look on the issue of slavery with greater tranquility. That was not to be the case. Pierce, a northerner, pursued the recommendations of southern advisers, and thereby hastened the entry into the Civil War.

During his term, the Kansas-Nebraska Act became law. It effectively reopened the question of slavery in the West. Southerners and people from the north rushed to Kansas to battle for control of the state. Open warfare broke out and Kansas became a forerunner to the Civil War.

In 1857, James Buchanan became our fifteenth president. He presided over a country that was becoming more and more divided on the issue of slavery. He was hopeful that the Supreme Court would resolve the issue via its ruling on the Dred Scott case. The Supreme Court's decision did little to settle the issue of slavery, and Buchanan left the slavery issue to his successor.

The Dred Scott case came before the Supreme Court in 1857. The suit had first been filed in 1846. Dred Scott was a slave of the Peter Blow family. The Blow family moved to Missouri in 1830. Missouri had been admitted to the Union as a slave state in 1820. The Blows later sold Scott to Dr. John Emerson, a military surgeon. Over the next twelve years, Scott accompanied Emerson to posts in Illinois and Wisconsin, where slavery was prohibited. The Circuit Court of St. Louis denied Scott his freedom, but allowed the Scotts (by this time Scott had married) to refile their suit. In the second trial, the court decided that the Scotts deserved their freedom, due to their years of living in the non-slave areas of Illinois and Wisconsin. However, the Missouri Supreme Court overturned that ruling. After a series of appeals, the case appeared before the US Supreme Court.

The Court ruled that Scott was to remain a slave. They ruled that, as a slave, he was not a citizen of the United States, and was thus not eligible to bring suit in a federal court. They further ruled that, as a slave, he was personal property and thus was never free.

It was a tragic and wrong-headed ruling. It defied the basic concept of why this country sought freedom. It ignored the fact that Dred Scott was a human being, and that all human beings are created equal in the eyes of their Creator. It denied the unalienable rights of life, liberty, and the pursuit of happiness. It proved that great danger lurks in providing the ultimate authority of law in the hands of a few people who are too frequently swayed by political motives, instead of the common sense application of natural and moral law when adjudicating our civil laws. It stood as the worst ruling of the Supreme Court for 116 years, until the *Roe v. Wade* case, which again ignored the reality of the existence of a human being. Both cases ignored the essential faith-based moral concept that all humans are created equal in the eyes of our Creator.

The Supreme Court, in the Dred Scott case, went even further in its blindness. It declared unconstitutional the provision in the Missouri Compromise that permitted Congress to prohibit slavery in the territories. It properly alarmed the anti-slavery people of the country and intensified the opposition to slavery.

The Dred Scott case and *Roe v. Wade* case stand as the worst governmental decisions in the history of this country. It is extremely unfortunate to have the judicial branch of government, which should be the ultimate recourse of all human rights, be so inept as to deny certain classes of humans the very fundamental rights of life and liberty. Those two cases will forever stain the history of this nation. Both decisions devalued one class of humans so another class could maintain some "greater" right. The right to force people to be slaves and the right to abort unborn humans will never be rights bestowed on us by our Creator. No Supreme Court, of this or any other country, should ever bestow upon itself such a right. The right to life is, and should forever be, a self-evident truth.

Abraham Lincoln became our sixteenth president, in 1861. It is not that often that the right man comes along at the right time in order to do the right thing. But that was true of the man referred to at various times as the Great Emancipator, Honest Abe, the Railsplitter, Old Abe, Father Abraham, or Uncommon Friend of the Common Man. Whatever title people called him, he was indeed a man of greatness who displayed a love for his fellow man, at a time when such love required great courage. He was born poor. He was born in Kentucky on February 12, 1809, in a simple log cabin with a dirt floor. He was not fond of his father, an itinerate carpenter, but was tremendously fond of his mother. He would frequently comment that everything he was, or hoped to be, he owed to his mother. His dedication to educate and improve himself has become folklore.

As a young man, he became interested in politics, but was not always successful in his attempts to run for public office. As his life progressed, he became increasingly opposed to slavery, and made it a cause to which he attached his political career. He became a national figure thanks to a speech he made in his home state of Illinois in 1854. In that speech, he stated that all national legislation should be enacted on the assumption that slavery was to be restricted and eventually abolished.

In 1858, Lincoln ran for a seat in the Senate, against Senator Stephen Douglas known as the "Little Giant" and who had a reputation as an outstanding orator. Lincoln proved to be his equal in that category. When Lincoln first decided to run, his campaign speech included the following words:

> *"A house divided against itself cannot stand. I believe this government cannot   e n d u r e permanently as half slave and half free. I do not expect the Union to be dissolved.---I do not expect the house to fall.---but I do expect it will cease to be divided."*

Lincoln and Douglas would engage in a series of seven famous debates having a great deal to do with the concept of "popular sovereignty" as advanced by Douglas. Douglas retained his seat by a narrow margin, but although losing the election, Lincoln increased his stature as a national figure, and the leading opponent to continued slavery.

In the presidential election of 1860, Lincoln became the nominee of the Republican Party. The Republicans were united in their assertion that slavery would spread no further. The election of 1860 had four major contenders for president. The badly divided Democrats had two candidates: Stephen Douglas from the north, and John Breckenridge from Kentucky, who was vice president at the time. The old Whig party, with membership primarily from the border states, nominated John Bell of Tennessee, under the new party label of Constitutional Union Party. Lincoln won only thirty-nine percent of the popular vote, but carried a majority of 180 electoral votes.

With the election of Lincoln, came the secession of South Carolina from the Union. South Carolina had been threatening to secede, and Lincoln's election was the excuse that helped them pull the trigger. Once the outcome of the election became certain, South Carolina, in a state convention, declared that the union existing between itself and other states under the name of the United States was dissolved. Within the next few months, and before Lincoln was sworn into office, six more southern states seceded, and adopted a provisional constitution to form the Confederate States of America.

In his inaugural address, on March 4, 1861, Lincoln refused to recognize the secession of the Confederate states. His speech was ignored by the southern states, and in April 1861, the Confederates opened fire on federal troops stationed at Fort Sumter in South Carolina, and so the Civil War began. The war would claim more lives of Americans on this country's soil than were lost in any other war.

Wars are never good wars, but the Civil War was fought to give an entire class of human beings the basic right of life endowed upon them by their Creator. In that regard, President Lincoln, and the men who died in that battle, restored the mantle of greatness to this country. Lincoln was a man who did not claim an affiliation with any specific religion, but demonstrated a faith-based morality that was not subordinate to any of our presidents. His lifelong dedication to the abolishment of slavery, despite the obstacles he had to overcome to achieve that goal, will forever establish his place in history as one of our greatest presidents.

CHAPTER 5---CIVIL WAR

Following the secession of the seven states, Jefferson Davis became president of the Confederacy. He soon became president of a larger Confederacy, as several more states seceded following the shelling of Fort Sumter. Virginia seceded and was rapidly followed by Arkansas, Tennessee, and North Carolina. When Virginia left the Union, it took Colonel Robert E Lee with her. Colonel Lee had been offered the command of the Union Army, but declined out of loyalty to his home state of Virginia.

Not all of the slave states joined the Confederacy. The border states of Delaware, Maryland, Kentucky, and Missouri, which had some sympathies to the South, nevertheless remained loyal to the North. People from those states often had soldiers in both the Union and

Confederate armies. This author grew up in the state of Missouri, and I still remember my grandmother passing on the stories of families who had relatives fighting on each side of the conflict.

Both sides in the conflict were hoping for a quick victory, but that was not to be. In resources, the North had an advantage. It had more factories to turn out the supplies necessary for war, and it had considerably more people. The northern states had a population of twenty-two million, compared with nine million in the south. The south had more experienced military leaders and had the advantage of fighting a defensive war on its home soil.

The first major battle of the war took place at Bull Run, Virginia, only a few miles west of Washington, D.C., and it was won by the South. That battle removed any hope that the war would be a short one for the Union forces. The southern forces were often victorious in battles fought along the eastern seaboard, whereas the Union forces had more success in the west, and in naval operations.

Major battles took place in the names now very familiar to those with interests in this conflict. Such locations as Shiloh, on the bluffs of the Tennessee River, were the scenes of bloody conflicts. More than 10,000 soldiers on each side were lost at Shiloh. Numerous attempts were made by Union forces to capture Richmond, the Confederate capital, but these were repeatedly denied victory, and the casualties were terrible. A second battle was fought at Bull Run where the Confederate army again was victorious.

The single bloodiest one-day battle occurred at Antietam Creek, near Sharpsburg, Maryland. On September 17, 1862, more than 4,000 died, and 18,000 were wounded. The battle at Antietam was inconclusive, but it had important consequences. Great Britain and France, who were about to recognize the Confederate government, delayed their decision following Antietam, and that recognition was never to be forthcoming.

Antietam also gave Lincoln the opportunity to issue the Emancipation Proclamation, which declared that as of January 1, 1863, all slaves in those states rebelling against the Union were free. Its immediate practical consequence was of little impact, but it did mean that the abolition of slavery was to be a specific goal of the conflict. The proclamation also authorized the recruitment of blacks into the Union Army. More than 200,000 African Americans would serve with the Union forces.

In the east, Lee's army continued to inflict losses on the Union Army. He was victorious at Fredericksburg, Virginia in December of 1862, and again at Chancellorsville in May 1863. With his victory at Chancellorsville, Lee moved into Pennsylvania. When he reached Gettysburg, a strong Union force met him. After a three-day battle in which more than 3,000 Union soldiers and 4,000 Confederate soldiers died, the Confederate Army was finally forced to retreat to the Potomac.

In November 1863, Lincoln traveled to Gettysburg to dedicate a new cemetery, and there he delivered the famous Gettysburg Address, which is repeated below:

"Four score and seven years ago, our fathers brought forth on this continent a new nation, conceived in liberty and dedicated to the proposition that all men are created equal. Now we are engaged in a great civil war, testing whether that nation or any nation so conceived can long endure. We are met on a great battlefield of that war. We have come to dedicate a portion of that field as a final resting-place for those who here gave their lives that this nation might live. It is altogether fitting and proper that we should do this. But in a larger sense, we cannot dedicate, we cannot consecrate, we cannot hallow this ground. The brave men, living and dead who struggled here have consecrated it far above our poor power to add or detract. The world will little note nor long remember what we say here, but it can never forget what they did here. It is for us the living rather to be dedicated here to the unfinished work, which they who fought here thus far so nobly advanced. It is rather for us to be here dedicated to the great task remaining before us --that from these honored dead we take increased devotion to that cause for which they gave the last full measure of devotion--that we here highly resolve that these dead shall not have died in vain, that this nation

under God shall have a new birth of freedom, and that government of the people, by the people, for the people shall not perish from the earth."

It was a great reaffirmation of our national adherence to a faith-based morality, and after eighty-seven years, the time had certainly come to have a new birth of freedom for those who had been under the bondage of slavery for too many years.

In the ending of his Gettysburg address, Lincoln duly noted the attributes of a national faith-based morality that restored a nation to greatness. He proclaimed, "that this nation under God shall have a new birth of freedom, and that government of the people, by the people, for the people shall not perish." When a nation applies those words to its actions, it truly exists under the label of a great nation.

More battles were yet to be fought. On July 4th, 1863, General Grant captured Vicksburg, Mississippi, which placed the Mississippi River in the hands of Union forces. The Northern victories at Gettysburg and Vicksburg turned the tide of the war in favor of the Union forces, but battles would continue.

After Grant's victory in Vicksburg, Lincoln made him the commander in chief of all Union forces, and in May 1864, Grant engaged Lee's Confederate troops in the three-day Battle of the Wilderness. In the west, Union forces gained control of Tennessee, which permitted General William Sherman to invade Georgia. After his success in Georgia, Sherman marched northward, and by February 1865, his army had taken Charleston, South Carolina.

While Sherman was advancing from the south, Grant laid siege to Petersburg, Virginia. Lee eventually retreated south. On April 9, 1865, he was surrounded by Union forces, and surrendered to Grant at the Appomattox Courthouse. Grant was a gracious victor and reminded his troops, "The rebels are our countrymen again."

In 1864, Lincoln was elected to a second term. In his second inaugural address to the nation, and with great eloquence, he stated what a great nation needed to do after a civil strife. His address spoke to the unknown works of our Creator, and his final words again noted the needs of a great nation: "with malice toward none, with charity for all, with firmness in the right as God gives us to see the right, let us strive on to finish the work we are in, to bind up the nation's wounds, to care for him who shall have borne the battle and for his widow and his orphan, to do all which may achieve and cherish a just and lasting peace among ourselves and with all nations." Lincoln not only endorsed the words of our founding fathers, his courage and his actions extended the unalienable rights to all citizens.

This nation shall forever be indebted to a great president.

Five days after Lee surrendered to Grant at Appomattox, Lincoln permitted himself the luxury of enjoying a performance at Ford's Theater with his wife. While seated in the presidential box, John Wilkes Booth murdered him. He was the first president of this country to be assassinated.

After the assassination of Lincoln, the task of bringing the states that had seceded back into the Union fell to the new president, Andrew Johnson. Lincoln's vice president was a Southerner who remained loyal to the Union. The Freedmen's Bureau was established in early 1865 to aid the former slaves in their need of self-support. Johnson also carried out Lincoln's reconstruction program. In December 1865, Congress ratified the Thirteenth Amendment to the Constitution, which officially abolished slavery. A monumental failure of this country to recognize the equality of African Americans who were kept in bondage was finally corrected.

This is a good point in history to review the human and legal reasons that one group of people could deprive another people freedom. Slavery was permitted to exist because the economic gains of many powerful plantations owners were dependent on slavery, and the people of the region accepted that. After a period of time, ignoring the human rights of others becomes ingrained in the culture of society. When one class of humans believes it has a greater right to equality than another group, faith-based morality is abused. Civil law is not always adequate to correct such abuse.

In the Dred Scott case, the Court believed that it was upholding the Constitution and the civil laws of the land. It forgot (or ignored) the existence of faith-based morality, which assumes that all people are created equal and are endowed by our Creator with the unalienable rights of life, LIBERTY, and the pursuit of happiness. The Court should have assumed that the absence of any civil law regarding the rights of human beings, who were slaves, merely meant that civil law was inadequate. One could probably argue that civil law was not inadequate even though the Court chose to believe that slaves had no rights as citizens and that humans could be defined as personal property. No matter who would win the debate on the adequacy of civil law at the time of the Dred Scott decision, we are in violation of faith-based morality when any of us, including the highest court of the land, choose to prioritize one class of humans over another.

In the opinion of this author, when civil law is in conflict with the morality derived from a faith-based view, it is always civil law that is inadequate. The Court in the Dred Scott case rendered a decision based on secular morality, and therein is the danger of such morality. It has no stable moral underpinnings, and it is dangerous for any country to base their laws on that type morality, which changes with the whims of humans. For two hundred years, slavery was a blemish on the greatness of this country.

CHAPTER 6---THE LATTER PART OF THE NINETEENTH CENTURY

Despite the abolition of slavery, the years following the Civil War were not necessarily kind to black Americans. In the South (and also many areas of the North), many whites found methods whereby white dominance was maintained over blacks. Supreme Court decisions, and the apathy of both political parties, did little to achieve racial justice. The Supreme Court has an unfortunate history of failing to establish the equality of human beings.

In 1873, the highest court of the country ruled that the Fourteenth Amendment conveyed no new privileges to black people. Ten years later, the Court did not prevent individuals from participating in racial discrimination, and in 1896, the Court ruled that "separate but equal" public accommodations (such as restaurants) did not violate their rights. Segregation extended into every aspect of life for African Americans. It was not only restaurants, but also railroads, hospitals, hotels, and schools that participated in discriminatory practices. Sad to say, such discrimination extended to churches. Churches, church leaders, and the laity are not immune from participating in secular morality.

Following the Civil War, the South remained one of the poorer regions of the country and remained largely an agrarian society. It too frequently tolerated racial violence, and politicians as well as the courts permitted it to happen. Following the Civil War and the abolition of slavery, it would take another one hundred years for the necessary legislation to remove the evil racial discrimination against African Americans. Despite many of the aforementioned shortcomings, the abolition of slavery was a major step forward

In the thirty-five years remaining in the nineteenth century after the Civil War ended, there was tremendous economic progress in this country. That period in history is a tribute to what free humans can accomplish.

When the Civil War ended, this country was primarily a rural society. It would remain primarily a rural society through the nineteenth century, but farming would be transformed from hand labor to mechanization. Before the Civil War, the McCormick reaper became an important machine for harvesting. It would soon be followed by equipment that would transform almost every aspect of farming. The output of American farmers increased substantially. Farming was no longer a labor of subsistence; it became a commercial endeavor. The combination of mechanization and the addition of vast new lands soon resulted in surpluses of farm products. The Morrill Land Grant College Act of 1862 also provided agricultural and industrial colleges, which would be centers of scientific research for further improvements in farm production.

To this day, the American farmer provides this country with a legacy to the freedom and hard work of motivated individuals when they are unhampered by excessive government intrusion. Unfortunately, in recent years, the government has found the agriculture industry an area in which their interference benefits the wrong people. The beneficiaries of government farm subsidies today too frequently are large corporate and individual farmers, who do not need the subsidies. Such is the outcome of lobbying efforts.

Even though this country remained largely agrarian during the latter part of the nineteenth century, it was gradually being converted into an urban society. With urbanization came new inventions that would provide many necessities and comforts of such a society. Technology brought the country telegraphy and the telephone. The typewriter, adding machine, and cash register became a part of the ever-increasing number of offices. New paper presses aided in the printing of the nations newspapers.

The nation in the latter part of the nineteenth century also saw the introduction of major steel mills. As urbanization grew so did the number of factories and workers. In the early days these factories had poor working conditions. The work was difficult and often unsafe and the hours were long.

Steel was not the only area of industrialization. Oil, lead, meat, tobacco, and sugar were all areas in which larger organizations such as corporations and trusts were becoming large areas for concentration of capital. Major corporations were also becoming involved in the areas of transportation and communications. Names such as United States Steel, Standard Oil, New York Central, and American Telephone and Telegraph would soon become household names.

The last half of the nineteenth century was a great period in the history of a great nation. The courage of our sixteenth president led to the elimination of one of the worst, if not the worst, injustice ever done to a class of human beings in this country. The hard work and creativity of free human beings led to this nation becoming a leader in agriculture and industry. It was a nation that generally adhered to a faith-based morality, and it proved that free people could accomplish many things. .

The presidents that served our country after Andrew Johnson, and prior to the twentieth century, are not generally listed among our greatest presidents, but their accomplishments (or lack thereof) merit a brief review.

Ulysses S Grant, the hero of the Civil War, became our eighteenth president, in 1869. His two terms in office did not represent a period of major change. Although a man of impeccable integrity himself, his administration was plagued with scandals, and he let some of the ills of Reconstruction in the South continue without much personal input.

Rutherford Hayes followed him. Hayes' election was close and disputed and finally decided in his favor by an Electoral Commission. Hayes made concessions to southerners and the radical reconstruction imposed on the South came to an end. Hayes was an honest individual and had a great concern for all people regardless of race or religion. His honesty helped restore a higher level of dignity to the office of the president. He had promised that he only wanted to serve one term, and he kept that promise.

For the next twenty years, a series of close elections were held, and between 1881 and 1901, no president served two successive terms, although Grover Cleveland did serve as the twenty-second and twenty-fourth president. Although earth-shaking legislation was not the order of that twenty-year period, other events were changing the nation.

As already noted, migration to the cities began after the Civil War, and the transition from an agrarian to industrial society had begun. This period in our history was proof that economic progress is not dependent on the heavy hand of government. The technology and industrialization of this country was a greater tribute to what free men are able to accomplish than it was to any great intrusive acts of government.

As businesses and factories grew, the need for larger amounts of capital also grew. Corporations and trusts became common in the new way business would be conducted. Some of the early major corporations have already been noted. The amalgamation of large businesses created substantial wealth for the stockholders, but many of the workers in the factories did not fare as well.

Although the factory worker of the late nineteenth century had a difficult life, many Native Americans had it worse. As expansion took place westward into the plain states and mountain states by farmers, ranchers, hunters, and miners, conflicts with the Native Americans grew. Conflicts occurred with many Indian tribes of the Midwest and West. The Sioux and Apache tribes were especially skilled warriors and often greatly resisted the settlers' migration. The Sioux dominated the plain states, and the Apache dominated the southwest territories.

The life of the Sioux was greatly altered by the diminishment of buffalo through the excessive slaughter of herds as settlers moved westward. Millions of buffalo were killed by the end of the nineteenth century, and in a few short years it had become an endangered animal in the country it had once roamed freely. Numerous conflicts occurred with the Sioux, who were led by such leaders as Red Cloud and Crazy Horse. Significant battles took place in the Black Hills of Dakota, on the Little Big Horn River, and later at Wounded Knee, South Dakota.

The Apache also offered substantial resistance to the settlers' migration into the southwest regions, and numerous conflicts took place until Geronimo, the last great Apache chief, was captured in 1885.

From the early years of the nineteenth century, government policy had been to move the Native Americans westward beyond the areas being settled. Eventually, the reservations became smaller and more crowded. The Dawes Act of 1887 reversed the previous policy and permitted the president to divide up tribal lands and parcel such land to settlers after it was held in trust for twenty-five years. Although some good intentions were associated with the new policy, it was disastrous for the Indian tribes, inasmuch as it took more land away from the tribes and further disrupted the Native American way of life. It would take another fifty years to correct some of the inequities of the Dawes Act.

In the latter part of the nineteenth century, European powers were building empires in Africa and also competing for trade in Asia. Japan was also developing into a foreign power, especially in the area of trade. The United States also began extending its sphere of influence beyond the mainland boundaries between the Pacific and Atlantic Oceans.

In 1867, the United States acquired Alaska from Russia. Many Americans were not impressed with the purchase, which was negotiated in large part by the then secretary of state, William Seward. With its arctic climate and few native residents, it was frequently referred to as "Seward's Folly." Approximately thirty years later, a different view developed when gold was discovered on the Klondike River and many American citizens traveled north to Alaska in search of riches. Many of them stayed.

The Spanish-American War of 1898 also extended the country's influence to the Caribbean and the Pacific. Cuba and Puerto Rico in the Caribbean and the Philippine Islands in the Pacific were controlled by Spain at that time. The combination of hostility at being controlled by Spain and this country's sympathetic view for their demands for independence were primary causes of the war. But as late as the mid 1890's, President Cleveland still wanted the country to remain neutral.

In 1898, during President McKinley's term of office, an incident occurred which triggered the war. The United States warship *Maine* was destroyed while tied up in Havana harbor. McKinley first attempted to remain neutral, but he ultimately succumbed to the demand for armed intervention. The war lasted only four months. Commodore George Dewey destroyed the Spanish fleet anchored in the Philippine Islands and Theodore Roosevelt led his "Rough Riders" to victory in Cuba.

In the treaty that the United States signed with Spain, the occupation of Cuba was transferred to this country. Puerto Rico became a territory of the United States and this country also occupied the Philippines.

The Hawaiian Islands also came under the influence of the United States in the latter part of the nineteenth century. Americans began developing the islands' resources shortly after the Civil War. In 1893, a new government was installed in the islands, which quickly asked to be annexed by the United States.

Overall, this country maintained a high standard of faith-based morality throughout the late nineteenth century. It was also becoming a global power. The country had abolished slavery, but racial discrimination had not been eliminated. Native Americans were not treated the same as settlers were, although efforts were made to integrate them into a new cultural paradigm. The culture was new and different, but the merging of cultures is always difficult. Freedom for individuals was not perfect but was improving.

For a government to maintain a high standard of morality, it must be faith-based, and the common denominator to measure compliance is the treatment of all humanity within a country. Faith-based morality also requires a delicate balance between religion-based and secular-based morality and that balance was being maintained.

As the country was entering the twentieth century, it was approaching 125 years of existence. That period of time may be an appropriate place to assess its progress along the lines of the alleged comments from Professor Tyler. A portion of that quote was as follows:

> *"The average age of the world's great civilizations has been two hundred years. These nations have progressed through the following sequence: from bondage to spiritual faith, from spiritual faith to great courage, from courage to liberty, from liberty to abundance, from abundance to selfishness, etc."*

After 125 years of existence, all citizens of this country had been delivered from bondage, most had a high level of spiritual faith and great courage, and all had liberty. It would be premature to state that by the end of the nineteenth century, it was a land of abundance, but it was moving in that direction.

Whether the words *spiritual faith* in the used quote have the same meaning as this author assigns to *faith-based morality* is uncertain. But this author does believe that many of us have spiritual faith without belonging to any specific religion. If spiritual faith means that a believer of such faith encompasses the belief that there is a higher power, which many of us refer to as God, as did our founding fathers, and that such a God has a better understanding of righteousness than humans are capable of understanding, then Professor Tyler and this author are somewhat in accord that such a belief is a part of faith-based morality. The other major requirement of faith-based morality is the belief that all humans are created equal and that we need to treat others as we wish to be treated.

Faith-based morality does not require that people belong to any specific (or even broad-based) religion. Expressions of faith-based morality have too often been confused with the specific word "religion" used in the First Amendment, especially by members of our judicial system. The distinction between the words *faith* and *religion* should be clear to our judges, but in recent years, the distinction has been blurred. The separation of church and state is appropriate, but the separation of faith and state is not. It is not difficult to understand that our First Amendment was silent on matters of faith. The Declaration of Independence and the Preamble to the Constitution had already established that we were a country founded on a faith-based morality.

For the first 125 years of its existence, this nation had a better understanding of faith-based morality and what it meant than is the case today. During that time period this country, with the exception of slavery, generally adhered to a faith-based morality and because it did so, it was a great nation. The twentieth century would bring many tests to its existence and its status as a great nation.

CHAPTER 7---THE EARLY TWENTIETH CENTURY

As the country entered the twentieth century, for-ty-five states had been admitted to the Union, and in 1900, William McKinley would be elected to his second term as the twenty-fifth president of the United States. Agriculture was still the primary business of the nation, but cities and corporations were growing rapidly. As farming became more mechanized and new lands were available for farming, production increased substantially in the late nineteenth and early twenti-eth centuries. Farm production was also increasing in the rest of the world, and the worldwide increases were causing price decreases in farm product prices. It was a problem that would continue for another century.

The life of the factory worker at the turn of the century was also difficult. Hours were long, wages poor, and work often hazardous. Women and children often made up a large part of the workforce in certain industries and their wages were even worse than those of the underpaid male adults. Very little of the wealth generated went to workers, and the judicial system far too frequently did not rule in favor of the worker. The lack of government intervention provided the impetus for other methods of reform. Early labor movements met varying degrees of success but too frequently were interested in moving to a more socialistic form of government. The American Federation of Labor (AFL) gradually replaced these movements. Samuel Gompers was the leader of the AFL and his motives were straightforward and less political. His goals were to increase wages, reduce hours, and improve working conditions. His efforts, and those of the AFL, would lead to an improvement for workers and the establishment of a large middle class of workers in our cities.

The plight of workers again demonstrated the weakness inherent in human beings who possess unrestrained power. Throughout the history of this country, the fallibility of people has been displayed through their greed and selfishness. Greed and selfishness has frequently collided with our national faith-based morality. When we justify slavery, discriminate against Native Americans, deny women the right to vote, or permit abortions, we only justify such actions via secular morality. Eventually, most of the blemishes on this great nation's record have been rectified, even though it has often been at too slow a pace. Slavery existed far too long and government shares much of the blame. The greed and selfishness of the late nineteenth and early twentieth centuries' financial barons lasted too long, as well. They deprived their workers of a justifiable portion of the financial benefits the workers brought them, and it took too long to enact labor laws. When enough citizens believe in a faith-based morality, they will eventually rebel against such injustices. If such injustices would be corrected with a constitution and laws based on secular morality is debatable, because it lacks the necessary moral foundation inherent in faith-based morality.

In September 1901, President McKinley was assassinated in Buffalo, New York, while attending an exposition in that city. He became the third president to be assassinated within a forty-year period. His vice president, Theodore Roosevelt, succeeded McKinley in office. The nation over which Roosevelt presided was a rapidly changing nation. It was now a nation of forty-five states and was populated from the Pacific to the Atlantic Ocean. It was rapidly becoming a world power. With industrialization and the growth of cities, some problems developed. Corrupt political bosses and corporate executives often ran cities and trusts that too frequently exploited workers and others. That climate gave rise to the call for reforms.

President Roosevelt presided over numerous reforms and it was obvious to him (and others) that many reforms needed to be made at the federal level. Laws were passed to improve the life of factory workers and to protect against the utilization and abuse of child labor. During his administration, government enforcement of anti-trust laws was improved, regulatory bills were passed which made the rates of railroads more equitable, and more power was put into the hands of the Interstate Commerce Commission. Laws were passed which made meat and other foods safer.

Roosevelt was also interested in the preservation of forestlands and initiated the national park system. The exploitation of the nation's natural resources was slowed so that future generations could benefit from the riches of this country. The popularity Roosevelt gained in the Spanish-American War, together with the acceptance of his progressive reforms and a charismatic personality, would have made it likely for him to win re-election in 1908. But, having served almost two terms, he decided not to seek re-election. He supported William Taft, a fellow Republican, who promised to continue the reforms of President Roosevelt.

President Taft did continue to implement reforms, but he angered many in his own party as he sided frequently with the conservative wing of his party. He opposed the entry of Arizona into the Union because he felt its constitution was too liberal. His conservative views led to a crushing defeat for the Republican Party in the 1910 elections. He angered his predecessor, and in 1912, Roosevelt opposed Taft for the nomination of the Republican Party, but was defeated by Taft in that endeavor. Roosevelt decided to run as a third party candidate and with the divisiveness that occurred, the Democratic candidate, Woodrow Wilson, won the election of 1912.

President Wilson was to initiate many changes during his presidency, but before those changes were implemented, two significant amendments were made to the Constitution in 1913. The Sixteenth Amendment authorized a federal income tax. It is hard to imagine that this country's federal income tax has been in existence less than 100 years. It would forever change the country, was the genesis for the growth of the federal government, and would be the financial support for what would eventually be hundreds of federal programs.

Shortly after the Sixteenth Amendment was ratified, the Seventeenth Amendment was passed. It would mandate that the people elect senators. At the present time, only the federal judiciary members of government are not elected, and the time may have arrived for a different way to select the members of the judicial branch of government.

During his first term, President Wilson would initiate many substantial reforms in the country. The Underwood Tariff Act, signed into law in October 1913, reduced the tariff on hundreds of items, which was long overdue. Late in 1913, the Federal Reserve Act was passed, which created the Federal Reserve Bank and System that was comprised of twelve districts. Prior to that time, the control of the money supply was in the hands of private banks. The Federal Reserve Bank has played an important role in maintaining a safe and flexible money supply and has been a significant player in making our economy less subject to excessive money supply swings.

Wilson also played an important role in getting Congress to authorize a Federal Trade Commission. The Clayton Antitrust Act was also passed and many of the abuses of major corporations were eliminated. Other changes also helped the working class. The Seaman's Act of 1915 improved living conditions for the workers on shipping vessels. The Federal Workers Compensation Act was passed, and an eight-hour working day was established for railroad workers.

The many reforms of the early nineteenth century undoubtedly helped the workers of the country and were important in creating a middle class in this country. One of the unfortunate downsides to the reforms was that the federal government would play an ever-increasing role in the life of Americans.

In the early part of the twentieth century, this country was a great nation. All citizens were slowly, but surely, reaping the benefits of freedom. Conditions for all Americans were improving. The Twentieth Amendment would be passed in 1920, giving women the right to vote. Racial injustices were still occurring, but the country had made great progress in not only ensuring the unalienable rights of life and liberty, but it was also improving the ability of all to pursue happiness through the federal reforms that had been implemented. It was becoming a land of plenty for all.

This may be an appropriate time to again look at the words of our Professor Tyler. In speaking of the world's great civilizations, he said:

> *"These nations have progressed through the following sequence: from bondage to spiritual faith, from spiritual faith to great courage, from courage to liberty, from liberty to abundance, from abundance to selfishness, from selfishness to complacency, from complacency to apathy, from apathy, from apathy to dependency, from dependency back to bondage."*

Hundreds of thousands of Americans died in the Civil War. The great courage demonstrated by our leaders and those fighting for abolition led to liberty for all. After that war, this country, through the hard work of farmers and those in the factories, began building a land of abundance. But it could not be said that such abundance had turned to selfishness. Most Americans were willing to work in an unselfish manner to provide abundance.

Professor Tyler also said:

> *"A democracy cannot exist as a permanent form of government. It can only exist until the voters discover that they can vote themselves money from the public treasury. From that moment on the*

majority always votes for the candidates promising the most money from the public treasury."

It cannot be said that by 1920 voters were voting for those who promised them the most money, because the elected officials did not yet have the ability to distribute large sums to the voters. However, some of the reforms of the early twentieth century, such as the Workers Compensation Act, and certainly the Federal Income Tax, would mark the beginnings of legislation that would ultimately lead to the power of federal elected officials to control, and be able to soon distribute, large sums to constituents.

Yes, we were a great country in the early twentieth century, but we had put into place the early legislation that would put greater and greater power in the hands of our federally elected officials, who would eventually control the distribution of a large financial amount of our gross domestic product.

CHAPTER 8---WORLD WAR I

As many reforms were being implemented during President Wilson's first term, the winds of war were blowing in Europe. The assassination of Archduke Ferdinand, heir to the Austrian-Hungarian throne, and his wife, Sophie, on a visit to Sarajevo, Bosnia, was the trigger that began the war, but many background factors were also involved in the war.

The greed and power involved in excessive nationalism and imperialism of numerous European countries contributed significantly to the beginning of the war. During the late nineteenth century and early twentieth century, numerous alliances were established among European countries, and many alliances also crumbled. Rivalry was great among the European countries in their pursuit of domination in Africa. As the European powers competed for domination, they also pursued a policy of building up arms. France and Germany greatly increased the size of their armies and England was intent on pursuing naval superiority.

Even before 1914, war almost broke out due to crises in North Africa and in the Balkans.

The assassination of the archduke set off a chain of events in Europe. The assassination took place on June 28, 1914. On July 28th, Austria-Hungary declared war on Serbia. Russia had already thrown its support behind the Serbians, and the Germans supported Austria-Hungary. When the Germans demanded that Russia demobilize, and Russia refused, the Germans declared war on Russia. The date was August 1, 1914. France would not commit its support to the Germans, and on August 3, 1914, the Germans also declared war on France. When the Germans attacked France via Belgium, which was officially neutral, England declared war on Germany. The date was August 4, 1914, only one day after the Germans had declared war on France. World War I was underway.

Was the war begun because of great crimes against humanity and freedom? Not really. The greed and power of governments and leaders of governments had much more to do with the war. The ugly hand of secular morality, via the lust for power, had struck. Soldiers would be killed and lands desolated in order for governments to achieve their pursuit of power. This war was not fought to serve any noble cause. Much could be written about the morality of this war as it relates to the European countries that were involved with it, but this book is intended to review the moral history of this country.

In the early years of the war, the United States remained neutral, but insisted that as a neutral country, it had the right to use the oceans for shipping purposes. Great Britain, and especially Germany, did not comply with President Wilson's demands for the right of shipping. Sentiments against the Germans increased in this country, when they sank the British vessel the *Lusitania*, which had more than 100 Americans on board.

Despite additional incidents, the United States stayed out of the conflict through 1915 and 1916. In November 1916, President Wilson was elected to a second term, largely because he kept this country out of the conflict.

In early 1917, Germany resumed submarine warfare, and the Germans sank five American vessels. On April 6, 1917, a large majority in both houses of Congress declared war on Germany. It was a war this country did not wish to fight, but events on the high seas finally forced us into the conflict. The moral reasons for this country getting into the war were different than most of the European countries. We entered the war because our rights as a nation were violated on numerous occasions.

In his address to a joint session of Congress on January 8, 1918, President Wilson enumerated his "Fourteen Points" as a basis for ending the war. Because of their significant legal, moral, and just reasoning, an abbreviated version follows:

1: *Peace covenants were to be open, and the*
    secret alliances that led to the war were to end.

2: *There was to be free navigation upon the seas.*

3: *There were to be as many removals as possible*
    of barriers to free trade.

4: *There was to be a reduction in arms by all*
    nations.

5: *There was to be an adjustment of all colonial*
    claims, and the interests of the people in those
    regions were to be given equal claims to the
    government involved.

6: *The Russian territory was to be evacuated,*
    Russia was to be left with its own
    determination of political development, and
    was to be given assistance from others in
    making that determination.

7: *Belgium was to be evacuated and given*
    sovereignty of its affairs.

8: *French territory was to be returned, and the*

wrong done in regards to the Alsace-Lorraine region were to be corrected.

9: *Italy's borders were to be adjusted.*

10: *The peoples of Austria-Hungary were to be permitted a free opportunity of development.*

11: *Rumania, Serbia, and Montenegro were to be evacuated.*

12: *The Turkish portion of the Ottoman Empire was to be assured sovereignty, but other nationalities under Turkish rule were to be assured security of life, and an absolutely unmolested opportunity of development. The Dardanelles were to be opened for free passage to the ships and commerce of all nations.*

13: *An independent Polish state was to be established.*

14: *A general association of nations was to be formed.*

The motives of the president excluded any forms of vindication or retribution, but rather, were a tribute to this nation's desire to seek peace among nations and freedom for all people involved or affected by the conflict.

In mid-1918, the tide of the war turned against Germany, and it requested that President Wilson seek a peaceful solution to the conflict, which would incorporate his Fourteen Points. Wilson obtained approval for such a peace from the Allies and on November 11, 1918, an armistice was signed.

The ideals contained in Wilson's Fourteen Points, which were the basis for achieving the armistice, proved impossible to be obtained in a final treaty. Wilson understood that some compromise on many of his Points would be necessary to obtain his goal of a League of Nations. But, by the time he was finished compromising, almost all of his Points had either been watered down or were ignored. He compromised almost everything to keep his dream of a League of Nations alive.

Wilson's Fourteen Points were truly idealistic and noble, but his negotiating skills and political prowess were lacking. He probably gave up on too many of his Points in order to preserve his desire for a League of Nations, and he made the political mistake of not involving the opposition party in his discussions. When the Republicans insisted on some changes in his proposal, he refused to compromise, and he was unable to achieve ratification of the League in his own country.

He then attempted to take his case to the people. While traveling in Pueblo, Colorado, the pressures of attempting to achieve the peace and ratification for joining the League of Nations took their toll, and Wilson suffered a severe stroke in September 1919.

He never fully recovered from the stroke, and without his strong leadership, the Senate did not approve either the Versailles Treaty, or this country's membership into the League of Nations. The Bolsheviks, which came to power in Russia, also did not approve entry into the League of Nations, and without the presence of the United States or Russia, the League never did achieve the stature President Wilson foresaw.

With the role Wilson played in obtaining the peace, combined with the role the United States armed forces played in helping defeat the Germans, this country became recognized as one of the most powerful nations of the world. It was not only a powerful nation at that juncture of its history; it was a great nation, which was adhering to the faith-based morality envisioned by our founding fathers.

It was a nation that, in the early twentieth century through many good reforms, built a strong middle class society, which was broader than any nation had ever achieved. It not only exhibited a great concern for the freedom and pursuit of happiness for its own people, but it also pursued that goal of freedom for citizens of other countries.

The Fourteen Points did not seek greater power or territory for this country. It sought freedom and peace for people throughout the world. It reaffirmed this country's belief that all humans are created equal and that they deserve the right to life, liberty, and the pursuit of happiness. It also demonstrated this country's belief that a proper national code of conduct depended on a morality that was grounded in the understanding that such a code was the extension of living within the wishes of a good and gracious Creator.

This country deserved the label of greatness throughout the first twenty years of the twentieth century. The end of World War I would bring this country into a new cultural and economic era.

<u>CHAPTER 9---THE ROARING</u> <u>1920'S</u>

World War I changed the world, and the United States, substantially. In Russia, the Bolshevik Revolution led to Communism under Lenin. Prior to the war, many of the European countries were governed by monarchies, but after the war, many countries turned to a republic form of government. There was a noted socialistic trend throughout the European continent.

In the United States, there was an economic boom, especially in the cities. Farmers did not benefit as much because a greater supply of farm products were available after the war and prices declined. After being led by Wilson and his pursuit of a moral peace, Americans became disillusioned with those lofty goals, and this country became more isolated from the rest of the world. Adding to the disillusionments was an epidemic that had broken out in Europe in 1917, which then spread to this country in 1918. Before it ended, a year later, more than 500,000 Americans had died. The post-war boom also was not long-lived as the economy returned to a more normal growth rate.

The country also suffered from labor unrest as workers became disenchanted with long hours and rising costs. In the year after the war ended, millions of workers went on strike. Race riots also occurred throughout the country. The citizens of the country were also concerned with the socialistic trends in Europe and especially the rise of Communism in Russia. The concern of the spread of Communism became known as the "Red Scare." It created enough concern that the attorney general set up a new department headed by J. Edgar Hoover. The concerns of the Red Scare never materialized.

The 1920 presidential election was, to a large degree, a protest vote against the idealism of President Wilson. The Republican candidate, Warren Harding, won a substantial victory. The 1920 election also included the votes of women for the first time. The long overdue right for women to vote was corrected with ratification of the Nineteenth Amendment.

The election of Harding led to a decided tilt toward creating a pro-business atmosphere. In the period of the 1920's, government operated on the basis that if business prospered, the rest of the citizens would also prosper, and that, in fact, happened. But, in its partiality to business, government went too far. It passed a series of tariffs that would eventually prove to be poor policy even though, in the short run, it gave many domestic companies a virtual monopoly and probably resulted in a short-term stimulus to business.

In August, 1923 President Harding, while on a trip to San Francisco, suffered a severe heart attack and died. His Vice-President, Calvin Coolidge, succeeded him. The country was enjoying economic prosperity as Coolidge took office. Coolidge did prove to be a more able administrator than his predecessor, whose administration suffered from the Teapot Dome scandal, which fully came to light after his death. Coolidge's first address to Congress included requests for tax cuts, limited aid to farmers, more economy by government and isolation in foreign affairs. He also maintained pro-business policies. From the time he took office until the presidential election of 1924 the country prospered and Coolidge enjoyed a great deal of popularity among the people. He was easily elected in the 1924 election with more than 54 percent of the popular vote. In his inaugural address he noted that the country enjoyed "a state of contentment seldom before seen" and he promised more of the same. He was a president who truly believed that if things were not broke there was no need to fix anything. He was also a man of few words. Although things were going well in the country he chose not to run for re-election in 1928.

The 1920's were a period of substantial change in this country. Cultural changes were taking place, and we were becoming a land of plenty. The reforms of the early twentieth century were paying dividends in the form of a better standard of living for many Americans.

With an expanded middle class made possible by the many reforms, we were indeed becoming a more affluent society. By the end of 1928, there were almost thirty million automobiles owned by Americans, which equaled one automobile for roughly every five citizens. Radios and consumer appliances were becoming commonplace. People in the cities were moving to the suburbs. With the new capability of industry to mass produce, and a growing affluent middle class to consume, the United States was turning into the richest society ever known to the world.

The 1920's was the era of the "Flappers," women who rebelled against the role that they had traditionally played in society. Their non-conformity and style of dress often shocked many citizens. It was also the age of jazz. Movies became popular and the first talking movie premiered in 1926. Broadway plays were in. The radio networks, NBC and CBS, were begun. Bing Crosby and other crooners became popular. With prohibition, came the "speakeasy." Prohibition also brought crime.

The 1920's, which was the greatest period of affluence experienced up to that point in this country, also brought some challenges to our faith-based morality. During the 1920's our government made significant changes in immigration policies. Immigration was at high levels in the late nineteenth and early twentieth centuries. In the first fifteen years of the twentieth century more than fifteen million people came to the United States. Many came from Southern and Eastern Europe, and included a large number of Jews and Catholics.

As a result of these immigrants, there was resurgence in the activities and membership of the Ku Klux Klan. With the support of many Americans, laws that limited the number of immigrants were passed. Too many Americans were spoiled by their abundance of freedom and prosperity, and were reluctant to share their good fortunes with others. That elitist attitude was attributable to a secular morality.

In some ways, the cultural clashes of the 1920's were not unlike those we are experiencing in society today. As life in the urban areas became more secular in the 1920's, many Americans sought out the older and more religious traditions. The major conflict of the cultural difference occurred in the 1925 trial of John Scopes, who went on trial for teaching evolution in a biology class.

However, the affluent period of the 1920's was not to have a long life. Many excesses had been building in the country. Even though the middle class had been expanding, it did not fare all that well during the

1920's. Real wages during that period increased very little and a large percentage of the population was living below the minimum poverty level. There was excess production in farming as well as the auto and textile industries. Broker loans on call rose dramatically from 1928 to 1929. Margin trading in the stock market was excessive. Only a small percentage of Americans were investors in the stock market and there was considerable speculation in stocks.

Where was Alan Greenspan when we needed him? His words "irrational exuberance" would have been appropriate in 1929.

After President Coolidge announced that he would not seek re-election in 1928, the Republican Party turned to Herbert Hoover as their candidate. He was nominated on the first ballot at the Kansas City convention. He brought with him an impressive background as an engineer, administrator, and humanitarian. During World War I, he served as head of the Food Administration. He managed to cut consumption of food, which was needed overseas, while also avoiding rationing. After the armistice, he headed the American Relief Administration and was instrumental in organizing shipments of food for starving millions in central Europe. He served as the Secretary of Commerce under presidents Harding and Coolidge.

Hoover proved to be a better administrator and humanitarian than prognosticator. At his acceptance speech in Kansas City, he stated the following:

> *"We in America today are nearer to the final triumph over poverty than ever before in the history of this land...We shall soon with the help of God be in sight of the day when poverty will be banished from this land."*

In the 1928 election, Hoover ran against Alfred Smith, who was nominated by the Democrats at their Houston convention. Smith was the first Catholic to run for the presidency. His religion was a major political issue. Accusations were made that if elected he would make Catholicism the national religion. Hoover won the election by a huge margin.

Was the United States a great nation during the 1920's? There is no doubt that it had become a powerful and prosperous country. However, there were also indications that prosperity brought with it a certain amount of secularism. The views on immigration, on religion, on excesses, and on bigotry were not trademarks of greatness. One can only wonder the direction the nation would have taken if prosperity were to have continued, but the month of October 1929 would change this country in ways that could not have been imagined during the roaring '20's.

CHAPTER 10---THE GREAT DEPRESSION

October 29, 1929 was the day the Roaring '20's came to a screeching halt. That was the day of the "Great Crash." During the month of October 1929, the stock market would lose approximately forty percent of its value. The ripple effect of the crash throughout the economy would be of catastrophic proportions.

President Hoover believed many of the early indicators of the depression were beyond this country's control, and he believed that confidence in our free market economy would be the solution to the problems. He initially believed it was important that businesses maintain employment and steady wages. However, as consumer purchases diminished, problems snowballed.

Factories and other businesses closed and banks failed. A major problem was that technology improved tremendously in the early part of the twentieth century (and especially after World War I), but the citizens of the country were not in the financial position to consume all the goods that were being made available.

As factories and businesses shut down, unemployment rose. No significant welfare system or other economic safety nets were in place in this country. Higher and higher unemployment led to poverty and hunger. Many people were forced to live in the shanties that sprung up around the country and were called "Hoovervilles." Hoover was indeed the scapegoat of the Depression.

Soup lines were set up by charities in many cities, but were not accessible to all. Never before, or since, had the country seen as much poverty, or as many suicides. By 1932, the unemployment rate had risen to twenty-five percent.

Hoover first believed that the free market would correct things, and he also believed in rugged individualism. However, as the situation worsened, Hoover began to take some action. Government did increase its spending on public buildings, roads, and dams in order to create jobs. A number of tariff acts, including the infamous Hawley-Smoot Act, were passed, but were offset by other nations countering with their own higher tariffs. These tariffs would create more problems as time passed.

Hoover also set up an emergency committee to advise local relief programs. In 1932, Hoover set up the Reconstruction Finance Corporation, which provided banks with government credit in order for them to extend loans to customers. How long the Depression would have lasted with some of the programs Hoover had initiated is a matter of speculation. But by 1932, the voters had enough. They elected Franklin D Roosevelt to the presidency by a huge margin.

Whatever else one can say about President Roosevelt, there can be no debate that he was a man of action. He believed it was necessary for government to take bold steps to end the Depression. He was about to utilize government programs in ways that would permanently increase the role of government in our daily lives, and in every facet of the economy.

President Roosevelt understood the importance of increasing the confidence of the American people. In his inaugural address, he told the citizens of the country that the greatest concern of the nation was fear itself. He made the decision to communicate with the people by a weekly radio address in order to assure them that recovery would soon be coming.

In his first few months in office, he initiated a myriad of programs aimed at stimulating the economy and providing relief to those who needed it, especially through the creation of jobs. No president has ever done more than Roosevelt in his first 100 days in office. His "New Deal" was a big deal. Most of the

New Deal programs were patterned after some of the social and economic reforms that were implemented in Europe after World War I, and he continued some of the reforms begun by the administrations of Theodore Roosevelt and Woodrow Wilson. What was different about the New Deal programs was the speed at which they were implemented.

He quickly addressed the sad state of affairs in the banking and credit system of the country. He ordered banks closed, and just as quickly, had banks that were solvent reopened. His policies were intended to include some moderate inflation in order to provide an impetus to commodity and other pricing, and also to give some relief to debtors. The Securities and Exchange Commission Act of 1933 created an oversight commission to protect investors, and tougher regulations were imposed on the sale of securities. Other agencies were also established which provided credit facilities to industry and agriculture.

Swift action was also taken to provide work for the millions who were unemployed. An early step was the establishment of the Civilian Conservation Corps (CCC). The CCC brought employment to young men between the ages of eighteen and twenty-five. The CCC workers were largely utilized in many jobs that conserved our natural resources and protected species of birds, fish, and game. The young men were paid about $30 per month. During the 1930's, the CCC employed almost two million workers at one time or another.

In November of 1933, further work relief came in the form of the Civil Works Administration. It created a variety of jobs such as highway repair. It was a short-lived program, but was a further indication that the Roosevelt administration believed it was better to provide relief through the creation of jobs than to give relief through direct welfare. The debate of direct welfare versus work welfare continues on today.

Organized labor also made great gains during the early years of the Roosevelt administration. In 1935, Congress passed the National Labor Relations Act, which gave workers the right to bargain through unions of their own choice, and prohibited companies from interfering with labor activities. The act also defined unfair labor practices and created the National Labor Relations Board, which would arbitrate unfair labor charges, and also supervise collective bargaining.

In 1933, the National Industrial Recovery Act was passed in order to end cutthroat competitive practices, and thereby create more jobs and more buying power. The act also established the National Recovery Administration. After a short period of time, business became disenchanted with the act, and in 1935, it was declared unconstitutional. By that time, other programs had been implemented to aid the recovery.

Business and labor were not the only ones hit by the Depression. Agriculture was also in the doldrums. In its belief that greater regulation could solve the problem, the Roosevelt administration and Congress passed the Agricultural Adjustment Act (AAA). The purpose of the act was to raise crop prices by subsidizing farmers for voluntary cutbacks in production.

From the beginning of the Roosevelt administration to 1935, farm prices had increased by fifty percent, but not all of that could be attributed to the AAA. During the 1930's, a severe drought hit the central farming states of the nation and severely reduced production. The drought would also create another miserable experience for the people of that era. Heavy winds and dust storms in the central farm states of Arkansas, Missouri, Oklahoma, and Texas became known as the "Dust Bowl." Thousands of people left the region to migrate to western states, primarily California. The Dust Bowl also provided the federal government with the reasons to establish the Soil Conservation Service in 1935.

The programs of the federal government would change the economy of the farmer. By 1940, almost six million farmers were receiving federal subsidies. The agricultural programs also provided loans on surplus crops, insurance for farmers, and a planned system of storage to ensure a stable food crop.

In 1935, a sea-change piece of legislation was enacted. On August 14, 1935, the Social Security Act was signed into law. The new act created a social security program, which was to pay workers age sixty-five (or older) an ongoing income after retirement. It also contained provisions for general welfare. Prior to the twentieth century, most of the population lived and worked on farms, and the welfare of elders was provided by the extended family. This arrangement changed as the Industrial Revolution provided more jobs for people in the cities. The Depression provided the final impetus for passage of the Social Security Act.

In the election of 1936, President Roosevelt won an easy victory over Alfred Landon, the Republican governor of Kansas. Roosevelt carried all states except Maine and Vermont. In that election, Roosevelt built a new coalition of Democrats, which would remain in place for decades. The coalition included labor, immigrants, urban ethnic groups, African Americans, and the South.

The New Deal legislation was a significant help in providing substantial increases in production and prices. However, the Depression was not over by the time Roosevelt began his second term. Pressures to deal with the ongoing unemployment problems brought suggestions and pressures from the right and left of the political spectrum. President Roosevelt's response was to propose a new set of measures to fight poverty, increase employment, and provide additional social safety nets. A major measure taken during Roosevelt's second term was the creation of the Works Progress Administration (WPA). As was true with other Roosevelt initiatives, it was intended to ease unemployment with work rather than direct welfare. The WPA would be responsible for new federal buildings, roads, airports, schools, and other federal projects. Another program, the National

Youth Administration (NYA) would provide part-time work and training programs for students. The combination of these programs provided employment and other assistance to millions of Americans.

The proponents and opponents of the many social programs of the first and second terms of President Roosevelt would be debated while he was in office, after he left office, and are still debated among historians and politicians to this day. There can be no doubt that the legacy of his programs had a profound effect on this country. The impact of his programs also had a subtle impact on the moral views of government and the purpose of government. For that reason, the moral consequences of the Roosevelt administration will be examined in a separate chapter of this book. But, the Administration of President Roosevelt was far from over in 1940, and would change significantly after his second term.

As Roosevelt was implementing programs to deal with the Depression in this country, other events were taking place, which were making the world a dangerous place. Totalitarian regimes in Japan, Germany, and Italy were becoming intent on expanding their regimes and spheres of influence. In 1931, Japan moved into Manchuria and set up a puppet government there. In Germany, Adolf Hitler came to power in 1933. He reoccupied the Rhineland and began building up his armed forces. Italy, too, had succumbed to fascism under Mussolini, enlarged its boundaries in Libya, and attacked Ethiopia.

During the 1930's, this nation underwent substantial political and governmental change, which, in turn, changed the moral attributes of the country. The Roosevelt administration substantially increased the social programs of McKinley, Theodore Roosevelt, and Woodrow Wilson. Because this book deals with our moral history, chapter twelve will deal with the impact the period of the Roosevelt administration had on our national morality.

CHAPTER 11---WORLD WAR II

Even as the clouds of war were encompassing Europe in the mid and late 1930's, most Americans were not inclined to have the United States involved in the conflict. This was a war of Europe, and the goal of our government was to stay neutral. That attitude remained in place as Germany, under Hitler, brought Austria into the German Republic, and occupied the Sudetenland of Czechoslovakia. With the armed invasions of Poland in 1939, and France in 1940, sentiments about the war began changing. Sentiments were with the democratic governments of Europe, and the sentiments increased as Germany began an air war against England.

This country began taking some defensive steps as it joined with Canada in a mutual defense pact and also made similar defense pacts with many of the nations in the Western Hemisphere. Large sums were expended by government to increase its armaments, and in late 1940, it passed legislation to create a draft of young men into the armed forces. The Lend-Lease program was also passed which gave President Roosevelt the right to provide arms to England, as well as to Russia and China. The program was intended to bolster the capability of those nations resisting the advancement of the armies of Germany, Italy, and Japan.

As war was spreading in Europe, the Japanese were becoming intent on bringing more countries in the Pacific under their influence. With England involved in the war in Europe, it was unable to resist the Japanese advancements, and it withdrew from Shanghai. Japan also occupied Indochina, and joined in a pact with Germany and Italy. The United States, in turn, imposed an embargo on the export of any scrap iron to Japan, which was needed for armaments.

In November 1940, Roosevelt won an unprecedented third term as president. His opponent, Wendell Wilkie, did not have any major disagreements with Roosevelt on foreign policy, and in 1940, the coalition Roosevelt had assembled during the Depression provided him with an easy victory.

During the period of the 1940 campaign, and following the election, the United States was in negotiations with Japan. The Japanese insisted on the lifting of embargoes and wanted the United States to stop naval expansion in the Pacific. Secretary of State Cordell

Hull, in turn, demanded that the Japanese withdraw from China and Indochina if the United States was to free any of the Japanese assets that had been frozen.

On December 1, 1941, the Japanese rejected the American proposal. On December 7, 1941, the Japanese attacked the United States Pacific fleet in Pearl Harbor, Hawaii. More than 2,300 military and non-military people were killed in the attack. Nineteen ships and about 150 planes were destroyed. On December 8, 1941, Congress declared war on the Japanese, and three days later, Germany and Italy, as members of the Axis with Japan, declared war on the United States. The United States, within a period of four days, became directly involved in World War II, on two fronts.

President Roosevelt mobilized the United States for war with the same rapidity that he employed to fight the Depression. Within weeks, he announced military production goals that were almost unbelievable in their magnitude. Tens of thousands of planes and tanks, along with staggering amounts of other armament, were to be produced in very short periods of time. Factories used for goods at home were rapidly converted to military production. Within a short period of time, the country had more than fifteen million people in the armed forces, and another fifty million employed in wartime production.

The dedication to the war was amazing. It had a leader in President Roosevelt, who achieved unbelievable results in short periods of time. It had a population that had endured hardships in the Depression, and who were as dedicated as any generation has ever been to the cause of freedom, and in their willingness to sacrifice in order to ensure that this country would remain free. They truly were a great generation. Could the results achieved in the years of 1941 through 1945 be accomplished today? In the eyes of this writer, who was an elementary school student at the time, the answer is no. We no longer have the dedication to freedom that the people of that generation had. Today, we expect such freedom, but are far less willing to do the things necessary to maintain it, in this country or abroad.

The United States, along with its allies, decided that the primary thrust of its actions would initially be in Europe, via Africa. The British forces were having some success in keeping the German general Rommel from pushing into Egypt. In late 1942, an American army landed in North Africa, and under General George Patton dealt some severe defeats to the German and Italian armies. During the same period, the Russians, after suffering severe losses, were able to defeat the German forces at Stalingrad.

By late 1943, the Allied forces had won victories in North Africa and in Sicily, enabling them to land on the Italian mainland. The Italian government would surrender unconditionally, but the German forces in Italy offered stiff resistance, and Rome was not liberated until the summer of 1944.

Under General Eisenhower, who was the supreme commander of Allied forces in Europe, plans were being made to open a western front against the Germans. On D-Day, June 6, 1944, the Allied forces landed on the beaches of Normandy in northern France. With forces commanded by Generals Patton and Bradley and others, the Allied forces liberated France, and then moved into Germany. Although the winter of 1944/45 saw some successful counter offensives by the Germans during the Battle of the Bulge, the Allied forces, by March 1945, had advanced far into Germany from the west, and the Russians did likewise from the east. On April 30, 1945, Hitler committed suicide and eight days later, the Germans surrendered.

After the initial attack on Pearl Harbor, and a defeat in the Philippines in early 1942, the Americans forces began having success against the Japanese. In April 1942, a fleet of bombers under General Jimmy Doolittle were able to penetrate Japan and bomb parts of Tokyo. Its symbolic value was of greater significance than its strategic value, but it did provide our troops with a significant moral victory. The Japanese were also planning an attack on Australia, but that plan was destroyed with the Battle of the Coral Sea, in which fighters from carriers dealt a significant loss to the Japanese. Battle after battle was waged along a string of Pacific islands, and the Allied forces, made up primarily of American and Australian forces, were successful in one amphibious assault after another.

In the fall of 1944, General McArthur, the commander of the Pacific forces, led a successful return to the Philippines. In the defeat of the Philippines, in 1942, McArthur escaped the islands with the vow that he would return. More than two years later, he would fulfill his promise with victory at the Battle of Leyte, and shortly thereafter, the Allies would again control the Philippines. By February of 1945, the Allies had taken Manila.

After a bloody, but ultimately successful, battle on the island of Iwo Jima, the Allies began attacking the Japanese mainland with a series of bombing raids on industrial sites, on airfields, and on other targets. By the time the victory in Europe had been won in May 1945, victory was also in sight against the Japanese, but the invasion by armed forces onto the mainland was calculated to lead to many Allied casualties.

As victories were nearing in Europe and the Pacific, President Roosevelt was elected to a fourth term in November 1944, when he again easily won the election over Thomas E Dewey. Roosevelt would not live to see victory in Europe or the Pacific. On April 12, 1945, our thirty-second president died. His vice president, Harry S Truman, who had first been elected to the vice-presidency in the previous election, succeeded him. President Truman had not been well briefed on the war by his predecessor.

As victory was being achieved in the Pacific, the new president was confronted with a monumental issue. If the Allied forces invaded Japan, hundreds of thousands of casualties were expected to be incurred. By that time, the United States had successfully tested the atomic bomb. It was Truman's decision that if the Japanese did not surrender, the atomic bomb would be used to bring Japan's defeat, thereby saving Allied lives. Before using the bomb, the Allies, at the Potsdam Conference, issued the Potsdam Declaration on July 26, 1945. In that declaration, the Allies promised the Japanese that their country would not be destroyed, nor would the citizens be enslaved, if they surrendered.

The surrender was not forthcoming, and on August 6, 1945, the first use of the atomic bomb was made on the city of Hiroshima. Two days later, a second atomic bomb was dropped on the city of Nagasaki. Although the atomic bomb undoubtedly saved many Allied forces lives and hastened the end of the war, the destruction of the bombs was horrific. On September 2, 1945, Japan finally decided to surrender. World War II had come to an end.

From 1929 through 1945, the United States had suffered through a terrible stock market crash, endured the Great Depression, and survived a world war. The impact on the people who lived through that period and the moral implications are numerous. The next chapter of this book will be devoted to the moral impacts of that period of time.

CHAPTER 12---MORAL IMPLICATIONS OF THE FDR ADMINISTRATION

It was the worst of times, but in many ways it was the best of times. The period of 1932 to 1945 was one of great suffering. First, the people endured the lengthy Great Depression, and then World War II. During that entire period, this country was under the leadership of one president, Franklin D Roosevelt.

During the Great Depression, the citizens endured numerous hardships, but people have a way of coalescing during difficult periods. Tom Brokaw of NBC referred to the generation that endured the Depression and lived through World War II as the "Greatest Generation." I totally agree with that assessment, even if our reasoning may be slightly different.

People of that era were not concerned with the cultural and value differences so frequently discussed in current times. Their concerns were with making a living during the Great Depression and maintaining freedom and liberty during World War II. The hardships of that time provided a deep fabric of moral fiber within society and people believed in the need of a good Creator to help them through troubled times. People had to make many sacrifices for themselves and their neighbors.

As a young child at that time, I recall that many meals included the wild berries we picked, the fish we caught, and the game we hunted. During the war, it was with a sense of patriotism that we hunted for scrap metal and rubber to assist in the war effort, and to have a few cents in our pocket. We understood the need to ration food, tires, gasoline, and other items because they were needed for the war effort. If protests occurred I neither saw nor heard them. As a young newspaper boy, I anxiously looked forward to the morning paper to see the progress General Patton and the Third Army was making. The Depression and the war did involve sacrifices, but the people understood the reason for them and made them willingly. Could the patriotism and sacrifice displayed by the citizens of that time be duplicated at this time? I doubt it. There is far too much apathy in this country today to repeat the effort made from 1932 to 1945.

It is hard to ascertain if the difficult times created the moral and civil strength of that generation, or if that generation was blessed with outstanding citizens who understood that the collective effort of all was necessary to move the country to a better and safer nation.

No matter the reason, it was a great generation, and it will always be with a great fondness that I recall the people of that era, and the contributions they were willing to make on behalf of others. It was indeed a generation who understood and practiced faith-based morality. That is not to say they were any more religious than people of other times, but their trust in God was unwavering as opposed to the secular views so common today.

During the entire period of 1932 to 1945, President Roosevelt led the country. He was the activist of all political activists. Whether one agreed with all his programs or not, one cannot deny that he was a man of action. When he took office, he believed that it was the role of government to take an active role in improving the lives of those who were suffering from the effects of the Great Depression. He may properly be accused of introducing socialistic programs, but if it is done for the temporary good of the people, it is difficult to debate the motives. If faith-based morality implies, and it does, that love of one another is of great importance, then Roosevelt demonstrated his faith-based morality by doing all he could possibly do for the benefit of all citizens. If future generations were to insist more and

ι ever bigger and better social programs, it does
ιssarily follow that the blame lies at the door-
step of President Roosevelt. We will never know how
long he intended all of his programs to last.

Roosevelt displayed the same inclination for action
in World War II that he displayed in dealing with the
Depression. The free world was fortunate to have the
leadership of Roosevelt and Winston Churchill at a
time it was desperately needed. These two men were
determined to preserve freedom for their countries and
their fellow human beings throughout the world. It is
easy to nitpick some of the details in how they accomplished their goals, but it is difficult to debate their motives.

This may again be a good time to look at the words
our friend Professor Tyler had to say about the likeli-
hood of a democracy to not survive:

> *"A democracy cannot survive as a permanent form
> of government. It can only exist until the voters
> discover that they can vote themselves money from
> the public treasury. From that moment on the
> majority always votes for the candidate promising
> the most money from the public treasury..."*

It may be that President Roosevelt's popularity was
in part due to his willingness to implement programs
during the Great Depression and during the war that
required large sums of money from the public treasury.
Nevertheless, there are times in history that such pro-

grams are appropriate. A government of the people, by the people, and for the people, must have an understanding that on occasion it must do extraordinary things for the people. If subsequent generations insist on social programs that may not be necessary and may require large sums from the Treasury, the blame lies with those who insist on such unnecessary largesse, and the subsequent politicians who legislate them. President Roosevelt did what had to be done.

During the 1930's, a debate took place in this country on the effects of the Roosevelt programs, as related to the subsequent consequences to the nation. In 1938, Roosevelt answered those concerns with the following comments made in a radio address to the nation:

> *"Democracy has disappeared in several other great nations not because the people of those nations disliked democracy, but because they had grown tired of unemployment and insecurity, of seeing their children hungry while they sat helpless in the face of government confusion and government weakness through the lack of leadership…"*

Roosevelt understood that a little socialism could be appropriate in dire times. As noted earlier, it may be that he can be blamed by some for too much socialism and setting a pattern of socialistic solutions when they may not be required, but he did what he believed was necessary for the times. When starvation of people is imminent and freedom is immediately at stake, worryhe impact on the future is not the highest

Let us now take a look at more of the quote attributed to Professor Tyler:

> *"The average age of a great civilization has been two hundred years. These nations have progressed through the following sequence: from bondage to spiritual faith, from spiritual faith to great courage, from courage to liberty, from liberty to abundance, from abundance to selfishness, from selfishness to complacency, etc."*

The generation living from 1932 to 1945 was one of great faith, great courage, and one that was willing to die for liberty's sake. They were not a generation that had a great abundance. That would happen later. That generation was truly a great generation. It may have been the Greatest Generation that this country will ever see. As noted earlier, it is doubtful whether society of today could respond in the same way. Abundance, complacency, and apathy may have become too engrained. The mixed attitude on recent wars we have fought for other people's freedom would indicate that to be the case.

Where was the country on the scale of greatness in the 1932 to 1945 period? By almost any measurement, it lived up to the faith-based definition of greatness. It was one of the greatest periods in this nation's history and would rank with the periods of the early days of this country and the period of the Civil War. The "Greatest Generation" made exceptional sacrifices during the Depression and during World War II. They not only sacrificed for themselves and their families, but they sacrificed for others in this country, and in the rest of the world. "No greater love has one than to lay down his life for another." The Greatest Generation did that time after time.

Where does President Roosevelt rank among the greatest of our presidents? He must surely rank among the greatest. His entire administration was one of confronting overwhelming problems. He confronted them with action. I am among those who believe his programs became a model of subsequent, excessive social programs, but I find no fault with most of the steps taken by Roosevelt. He fits comfortably in my definition of those who are guided by faith-based morality. How he communicated with his Creator, I do not know, but his concern for his fellow human beings was demonstrated again and again and again.

CHAPTER 13---POST-WAR AMERICA AND THE COLD WAR

Harry Truman, our thirty-third president, as noted earlier, was not well briefed by his predecessor, nor did he feel well prepared for the enormous task he inherited. However, Truman also proved to be a man of action. His decisions to end the war in the Pacific were bold and decisive. The end of World War II did not bring an end to problems at home or in the world.

Truman's first priority after the war was to transition the United States from a wartime to a peacetime economy. Considering the number of members who had been in the armed forces, and the other non-military people dedicated to the war effort, the transition was not an easy chore. The G.I. Bill that was passed before the war ended, helped returning servicemen to obtain an education and loans to purchase a home.

Even with the G I Bill, servicemen found considerable competition for jobs. The result was considerable unemployment and labor unrest. During the war, people understood the need to sacrifice, but after the war many felt they deserved better pay increases. The result was labor unrest, and in 1946, over 4.5 million people were on strike at one time or another, which was a record for this country. Many major industries were affected including automobiles, steel, railroads, coal, and others.

Shortly after the war ended, Truman had proposed a twenty-one-point program to get the economy moving. His proposals included a higher minimum wage, greater unemployment compensation, federal housing assistance, increased unfair labor practices, and a number of other steps. The program was well intended, but may have been excessive considering the short period of time during which proposals were made.

Republicans felt Truman's programs were too expensive, and an excessive approach. They believed it was time to cut spending and taxes, and in the 1946 elections, they became a majority party in both houses of Congress. During the following two years, Truman's battles with the Republican Congress were legendary. Truman ran for re-election in 1948, and despite polls that had him behind Thomas Dewey, the Republican candidate, he won a stunning victory.

Despite some of the aforementioned transitional problems, the American economy was expanding rapidly after the war. The pent-up demand created by the war provided significant growth in the economy. During the 1940's, the gross domestic product of the country grew fifty percent. The large number of returning servicemen and women created a housing boom. The automobile industry that produced military armament during the war years turned out a record number of vehicles. We were becoming a land of plenty.

Although the war was over, another threat soon began surfacing. Totalitarian Russia was attempting (and succeeding) in expanding its sphere of Communist influence. During the closing months of World War II, the Russian army had occupied many of the countries in Eastern and Central Europe. In country after country, the Russian army assisted in setting up puppet Communist governments. In 1946, Winston Churchill coined a phrase with which most people of the world would become familiar. He said an "Iron Curtain" has descended across the continent. He further stated that the United States and Britain had to work together to stop the Soviet threat. Containment of the Soviet Union and Communism became policy.

In late 1946 and early 1947, Greece and Turkey were threatened with in-roads from Communism. In response to that threat, Truman declared a policy that became known as the Truman Doctrine. That policy stated that the United States would support free peoples who were resisting subjugation by outside pressures. To aid in keeping countries free, he asked Congress for an appropriation of $400 million. Congress approved the request.

The Soviet Union posed another threat to the free world in 1948. After the war, Germany was divided into four zones, the United States, England, France, and the Soviet Union. The city of Berlin was also divided into four zones. The United States, England and France, which controlled western Germany, discussed placing their zones into a consolidated zone. The Soviet Union, which had opposed any consolidation of Germany, responded by blockading Berlin, cutting off all ground routes into Berlin.

Fearful that the fall of Berlin could be a threat to all of Germany and the rest of Europe, Truman responded by ordering a massive airlift into Berlin. England and France joined in the effort. More than 270,000 flights airlifted massive amounts of food and other supplies into Berlin. After 231 days, the Soviet Union lifted the blockade. A severe threat to Germany and Western Europe had been stopped.

With the never-ending threats from the Soviet Union, and at the urging of the United States, the North Atlantic Treaty Organization (NATO) was formed. Eleven countries, plus the United States, joined NATO. Under the NATO treaty, any attack against one of the nations of NATO was to be considered an attack against all the member nations, and such an attack would be met with appropriate force.

During the war, representatives of twenty-six countries pledged the support of their governments to fight the Axis powers. President Roosevelt first used the name "United Nations" for this group of countries. The twenty six countries signed the "Declaration by United Nations" on January 1, 1942. The United Nations, as we know it today, was chartered on June 26, 1945, and it originally included fifty-one countries. It officially came into existence on October 24, 1945. Its role as a world peacemaker has been the subject of debate in this country.

The United States, in the late 1940's, was confronted with numerous challenges in Europe, but Asia, too, presented problems during Truman's administration. In China, the nationalist government, under Chiang Kai-shek, was fighting not only the Japanese, but also an internal threat from the communist leader, Mao Zedong. In 1949, Mao was successful in gaining control of China, and he aligned himself with the Soviets in their pursuit of communist influence throughout the world.

After the war had ended, the country of Korea, which had been liberated from the Japanese, was divided along the thirty-eighth parallel. The North came under the control of the Communists, and the South's government was aligned with the United States. The tensions between the Soviet Union and the United States were also felt between the two Koreas. In June 1950, the North Koreans invaded the South, which drew the United States into the war. Truman entered the war because he perceived the invasion as a threat to global security. The justification for entering the war was not much different than would be used later to justify the entry into the Vietnam conflict, but in 1950 the attitude of most of the country was that the threat from communism justified such action.

Truman decided not to seek re-election in 1952, and the country turned to one of the major heroes of World War II to lead the country. Dwight D Eisenhower's popularity from the war carried over to 1952, and he easily defeated the Democratic nominee, Adlai Stevenson.

In personality, Eisenhower contrasted significantly from Truman. He approached things in a "laid back" manner versus the "rapid fire" approach of his predecessor. Early in his administration, the Korean conflict became stalemated, and an agreement was signed, which established boundaries in much the same place as they were at the beginning of the war.

Although they differed in style, Eisenhower's foreign policy was not much different than Truman's. Containment of communism remained a high priority. "Ike" believed in a conservative policy for fiscal affairs and a liberal policy for people affairs.

In the fifteen post-war years under Truman and Eisenhower, the country experienced substantial economic growth. The Gross National Product, the measure then used to determine the amount of goods and services produced, grew at a rapid rate. As noted earlier, there was a substantial increase in the production of automobiles and other goods. There was a pent-up demand for housing, and a housing boom continued through the entire fifteen-year period. As farms consolidated, more and more people who had lived on the farm migrated to the cities.

Not only was there a large increase in the number of jobs, but the jobs were also better. Productivity gains made it possible for more and more goods to be produced with fewer workers, and the number of white-collar jobs increased substantially. With corporations becoming larger, more people were becoming part of management. The middle class of the country was growing rapidly. In the period from 1945 to 1960, this country truly became a land of abundance and undoubtedly the richest nation in the world.

In the sequential steps of our friend, Professor Tyler, we had undoubtedly moved along his chain of steps from a country of liberty to a country of abundance. Would it lead to a country of selfishness? We will examine that question in the subsequent pages of this book.

This country was a great nation in the period of the Depression, through World War II, and for the fifteen-year period following the war. That thirty-year period was a great period in this nation's history. It was a powerful nation, and a nation that demonstrated a faith-based morality in its concerns and actions for its own citizens and for the citizens of other countries. Faith and sacrifices were made by many for humanity, and for freedom's sake. It was indeed a nation that had malice toward none and sought justice and liberty for all. It was a country that was unified in that belief for thirty years.

CHAPTER 14---THE 1960'S AND '70'S: A DIFFERENT MORALITY

In 1960, John F Kennedy narrowly defeated Richard Nixon to lead our country. Kennedy was the first Catholic to hold the office of president of the United States, and the youngest man to hold the office. He was a charismatic man and a hero of World War II. He gave an electrifying inaugural address in which he asked the people of our country to ask not what the country could do for them, but rather what they could do for the country. He was unaware that he was about to lead a country whose citizens were going to do the opposite of his request.

During Kennedy's time in office, the Cold War had its most dangerous episode. Fidel Castro, who had taken over Cuba, told the world that he was a Communist and was aligning his country with the Soviet Union and China. The Soviet Union began supplying arms to Cuba, and in October 1962, aerial photos indicated that missiles were being installed that could launch atomic warheads against the United States, and the surrounding region. Kennedy ordered a blockade of Cuba and insisted that the Soviet Union remove the missiles. After several tense days, the Soviet premier ordered that the missiles be withdrawn. World War III was averted.

President Kennedy also sought greater equality for African Americans, and had to call on the National Guard on two occasions to protect blacks who were seeking to integrate schools. Kennedy also promised new social legislation that he referred to as the New Frontier. Before much of that program was enacted, the young president, while on a speaking tour, was assassinated in Dallas, Texas, on November 22, 1963. Lyndon Johnson became the eighth vice president to succeed to the presidency.

Lyndon Johnson was a former majority leader of the Senate and a highly skilled politician. He described his vision of social programs as legislation that would create a "Great Society." He was successful in passing many of the programs. The legislation he managed to get through Congress included large federal aid to education, anti-poverty programs, the Medicare program for people over sixty-five, and new civil rights legislation.

Johnson was able to guide much of his domestic programs through Congress, but he would have far less success in foreign affairs, especially with the war in Vietnam. As early as the late 1950's, North Vietnamese guerillas began attempting to overthrow the non-Communist government in South Vietnam. Under presidents Eisenhower and Kennedy, the United States sent military supplies and advisers to help the South Vietnamese government. President Johnson, in an effort to end the conflict, began sending troops to fight alongside the South Vietnamese army. The war had serious consequences in this country, with many people opposed to the war and insisting that our troops be removed. Johnson refused, and when the war became more entangled, Johnson decided not to run for another term in 1968.

The war was just one of many tragic events of the 1960's. President Kennedy had been assassinated in 1963. In April, 1968, Martin Luther King, Jr., the African American leader of the civil rights movement, was assassinated in Memphis. Two months later, Robert Kennedy, the younger brother of President Kennedy, who was campaigning for the Democratic presidential nomination, was assassinated in California.

After the assassination of Robert Kennedy, the Democrats turned to Johnson's vice president, Hubert Humphrey, to oppose Richard Nixon, who eight years earlier had lost a narrow election to John F Kennedy. A number of factors led to a narrow victory by Nixon.

Anti-war sentiment and protests that were violent led to a chaotic Democratic convention in 1968 that left the party divided. A backlash to the civil rights legislation permitted George Wallace of Alabama, who ran on the American Independent Party ticket, to carry five southern states. Nixon also promised to get the United States out of the Vietnamese conflict, and to restore law and order in the United States which had become home to numerous and sometimes violent protests against the war.

Nixon began withdrawing troops from Vietnam, but stepped up other tactical aspects of the war. His national security adviser, Henry Kissinger, finally managed to negotiate a cease-fire in 1973, but the war lingered on, with the North Vietnamese finally taking control of all of Vietnam in 1975. Whether the government was at fault for fighting a war to which it was only partially committed, or whether the citizens of the country were at fault for lacking interest in the freedom of other people, is hard to determine, but it was an unpopular war that this country lost. The reasons for becoming involved in the conflict were not much different than the Korean War, but, Americans had become less willing to be involved in fighting for the freedom of other people.

Nixon did have some success in foreign policy. He was able to open some ties with the Communist regime in China and was also successful in pursuing his policy of "détente" with the Soviet Union. He was able to negotiate the Strategic Arms Limitation Treaty with the Soviet Union that led to the reduction of nuclear arsenals and anti-missile systems.

Nixon was easily re-elected in 1972. Shortly after the election, the Watergate incident surfaced. A group of Republican political operatives had broken into the Democratic offices in the Watergate complex along the Potomac River. The scandal ultimately led to Nixon's resignation from office before he would have removed by the Senate. He was replaced by Gerald Ford, who had become Nixon's vice president following the resignation of his elected vice president, Spiro Agnew. Politics had become an ugly game.

Gerald Ford helped restore some faith in government, but during his time in office, the country entered a severe recession that would linger on for several years. In 1976, Jimmy Carter, who had been the governor of Georgia, defeated Ford. Carter's domestic policies were mixed and did little to cure the combined domestic ills of high unemployment and high inflation.

Carter's foreign policy achievements were also mixed. He did broker a peace settlement between Israel and Egypt. He also obtained Senate ratification for the return of the Panama Canal to Panama and he gave formal diplomatic recognition to the People's Republic of China.

On the other side of the equation, his insistence on an "absolute" commitment to human rights was an irritant to the Soviet Union. In 1979, after he gave asylum to the former Shah of Iran, angry Iranian militants seized the American embassy in Tehran, and held fifty-three Americans captive until the day Carter left office.

It is doubtful that the period of 1960 to 1980 will go down as a great period in this country's history. It will certainly not go down as a great period in the opinion of this writer:

It was a period during which government provided poor leadership and burdened the country with excessive programs.

It was a period during which the Supreme Court participated in the devaluation of humanity.

It was a period during which citizens became apathetic toward the freedom and liberty of others.

It was a period during which the best of traditional values were discarded, and the country turned away from a faith-based morality to secular morality.

It was a period during which the decay in morality led to a breakdown of the traditional benefits of marriage and the nuclear family.

It was a period during which sexual freedom, pornography, obscene language, and gestures became parts of our landscape.

It was a period during which the role of many major groups in our society became conduits of secular morality.

It was a period during which we moved from abundance to selfishness, apathy, and complacency.

It was a period that demonstrated the "Greatest Generation" had sired the "ME Generation."

It is only fair that this author give a few of his reasons for the indictments included in the above statements, and of his opinion why the greatness of this country was substantially diminished during the period of 1960 to 1980:

From 1960 to 1980, the government began promising and providing more and more social programs. The New Frontier and Great Society programs were intended to place government into the lives of those who "needed" government help. The "War on Poverty" program implemented during the Johnson administration was to eliminate poverty by improving the living conditions of poor people and enabling them to find their way out of the cycle of poverty. The food stamp program was one of forty programs included in the War on Poverty. Did they put an end to poverty? No! Will they put an end to poverty? No!

Government welfare programs, with no recompense from recipients through community service or other work, are crutches, not cures. Government's job is to ensure freedom and liberty and the right to the pursuit of happiness, but it cannot ensure, via legislation, that people will pursue those rights. It cannot guarantee that citizens will be hardworking and willing to sacrifice to achieve personal goals. We need to help the poor, but we need a better way to do it. Welfare must include responsibility and accountability, and therefore it must involve some type of payback for the assistance received.

The Great Society program also included sixty bills to improve education. Programs provided for new and better-equipped classrooms, low-interest student loans, minority scholarships, and a host of other "improvements." Have education results improved? No!

It is a ludicrous and doomed concept to believe that our centralized federal government can somehow be the catalyst for improving the education of children attending school in Hermann, Missouri; Orofino, Idaho; Warren, Arkansas; or any other small town or city in this country. Education for our children would be far better served if the federal government removed itself from any involvement

117

in education and left that responsibility to local communities, where it belongs. The ability of the federal government to improve education is not only a ludicrous concept, but the American people must also pay useless taxes to perpetuate it.

The above examples are only two programs where the government has over-promised and under-delivered. If the employee and employer contributions to Social Security had been invested in the same manner as private pension funds and guaranteed by the federal government, the payments to retirees today could be at least twice the amount they actually are. Our senior citizens deserve a safety net in their retirement years, and they are being short-changed by the lousy returns they receive on the funds that they and their employer have paid on their behalf. The idea of a mandated retirement safety net is sound, but it has been poorly executed.

In 1973, the Supreme Court rendered its decision in *Roe v. Wade*. That decision sanctioned the killing of unborn human beings. It was a genocidal decision and permitted the devaluation of humanity as Hitler had permitted thirty years before. It ranked with the *Dred Scott v. Sanford* decision that was also void of any faith-based morality.

The decision of this government to become involved in the Vietnam War was not unlike the justification to get involved in the Korean War. It was government's view that the curtailment of Communism was essential to the good of the world and that freedom was not forthcoming under totalitarian Communist governments. At that point in our history, we were no longer a society that was concerned with the freedom and liberty of others. We had become complacent in our pursuit of life, liberty, and happiness for anyone other than ourselves. I would ask of those who were so vehemently opposed to the Vietnam War if they believe the citizens of South Korea have less to be thankful for than the citizens of South Vietnam, Cambodia, or Laos. Freedom for those citizens was of minor consequence to those protesting the war.

The 1960 to 1980 period was an era of objection to traditional values without consideration of the merits of those values. No agenda for a higher set of faith-based values was forthcoming. Rather, we had an increase in drugs. We had a hippie culture that had a motto of "tune in, turn on, and drop out," as if that somehow would benefit society. We had a breakdown of the traditional nuclear family and became more obsessed with sexual freedom, pornography, and foul language. Secular morality was replacing faith-based morality.

Some minority groups and women were beginning to demand appropriate equal rights, and that was one of the good things that happened in that era. Other groups, including the media, were not serving society. Rather, they were becoming advocates of positions that too were grounded in secular morality.

The "Greatest Generation" in our history had sacrificed much to preserve freedom and liberty in our country and much of the rest of the world. As parents, that generation had shortcomings. They sired the "Me Generation" which often scorned the accomplishments of the generation of their parents. They were the generation that moved our society from one of courage and abundance, to one of selfishness, apathy, and complacency. They contributed very little to what had been a great nation. They continue to contribute very little.

A better understanding of that era may be provided by taking another look at the words of our Scottish friend, Professor Tyler:

> *"A democracy cannot exist as a permanent form of government. It can only exist until the voters discover that they can vote themselves money from the public treasury. From that moment on the majority always votes for the candidates promising the most money from the public treasury."*

I do not know if a majority of the citizens of this country now believe that their lives can best be improved by government promises and expensive government programs, but we certainly began moving in that direction at an accelerated pace beginning in the 1960's. Government is now more concerned with social programs that redistribute wealth than they are with the freedom that permits citizens the opportunity to pursue wealth on their own merits.

The latter part of Professor Tyler's opinion states:

"These nations have progressed through the following sequence: from bondage to spiritual faith, from spiritual faith to great courage, from courage to liberty, from liberty to abundance, from abundance to selfishness, from selfishness to complacency, from complacency to apathy, from apathy to dependency, from dependency back to bondage."

Not everyone, but far too many of us became selfish, complacent, and apathetic in the 1960's and 1970's. President Kennedy's request of ask not what your country can do for you, but instead what you can do for your country seemed not to have left a great impression on the ME Generation.

Faith and sacrifice, love of Creator, kindness, and consideration for our fellow human beings was replaced by a drift to the secular morality notions of, "Me first and everyone else later. Let government collect more taxes, as long as I get the lion's share, or think I may get the lion's share." We may have been one of the powerful nations of the world from 1960 to 1980, but we were no longer a great nation. We began succumbing to the notion that socialism is more attractive than individual freedom.

It would be an overstatement to classify everyone in the Greatest Generation as a great human being, just as it would be to state that all in the Me Generation were absorbed with Me. Nevertheless, as a collective group, the Greatest Generation, through sacrifice, love of country, love of freedom, and love of fellow human beings, was a group who demonstrated a high level of faith-based morality. That simply was not the case with the Me Generation. The Me Generation did not go away after 1980.

CHAPTER 15---THE FINAL YEARS OF THE TWENTIETH CENTURY

On January 20, 1981, Ronald Wilson Reagan was sworn in as this country's fortieth president. His term of office began after this country experienced twenty difficult years. It appeared that the difficult period would continue, when after only sixty-nine days in office, an assassination attempt was made on the life of the fortieth president. His charisma, wit, and optimism during his rapid recovery would become trademarks of his presidency, and immediately increased his popularity with the citizens of this country.

Reagan was a man of humble beginnings. He worked his way through a small college in Illinois, and then became a sports announcer. In 1937, he took a screen test through which he achieved a contract in Hollywood. He would appear in more than fifty films in the ensuing two decades. Toward the end of his acting career, he became president of the Actors Guild, and during his term in that role his political views became more conservative.

He became active in politics, and in 1966, he was elected governor of California, and was re-elected in 1970. Following an unsuccessful run at the presidency in 1976, he won the nomination of the Republican Party in 1980, and in that election handily defeated the incumbent president, Jimmy Carter.

Reagan was not a complex man. He believed strongly in a few simple economic and foreign affairs principles. He believed in a limited role for the federal government, a reduction in taxes for the American taxpayers, and a foreign policy that pursued peace through strength. He pursued those goals through a skillful communications style, honed by his years as an actor, and with an optimism and wit rarely seen in the oval office.

He was successful in achieving much of his legislative goals, despite a Congress in which the opposition party controlled both the House and Senate. He refused to deviate from his legislative agenda, even when his increase in defense spending contributed to larger deficits. His optimism was infectious with the American people, and the renewal of the people's confidence in government led to an easy victory for Reagan in 1984.

In his second term, he was successful in achieving a treaty with the Soviet Union, which would eliminate intermediate-range nuclear missiles. This treaty, his continued belief in peace through strength, and his personal relationship with Mikhail Gorbachev, the Soviet leader, would lead to the removal of the Iron Curtain of Communism that had been raised more than forty years earlier.

Ronald W Reagan was a great president and a great man. With a unique charm and an optimistic spirit, he epitomized the characteristics of faith-based morality. He would have been a wonderful associate and cheerleader in the room in which the Federal Convention had gathered 200 years earlier when the Constitution was signed. He truly ranks with our greatest leaders.

Despite all he achieved, some ills remained in our society. Despite Reagan's belief that human life began at conception and that abortions were wrong, their legal permissibility continued. The secular morality notions of individual freedoms for actions such as pornography, greater and greater emphasis on sexual freedom, and an increase in vulgar language in music and other media continued. The breakdown in marriages also continued.

A great leader could not overcome the ills brought to us by the Me Generation.

George H W Bush, Reagan's vice president, became our forty-first president in 1989. He believed in and continued the programs of his predecessor. He, too, was a man of great integrity. He had a distinguished record of service to his country during World War II and in numerous other political and governmental positions before being elected president.

In domestic affairs, Bush had promised no new taxes in his 1988 campaign. For two years, he maintained that policy, but with large deficits continuing, Bush did include some proposed tax increases in 1990. Even if tax increases were appropriate at the time, the breaking of a promise to voters is always risky business, and it would hurt him in the 1992 election.

In foreign policy, the Bush administration accomplished a great deal. After Reagan's success in dealing with the Soviet Union, Bush, too, was successful. In 1991, the United States and Soviet Union signed the Strategic Arms Reduction Treaty. That agreement, and the symbolic tearing down of the Berlin Wall that separated East and West Berlin, were the final episodes of the Cold War.

As the Cold War was ending, another area of the world was posing a danger. In August 1990, Iraq invaded Kuwait. A number of resolutions were passed in the United Nations condemning the invasion. After they were ignored by Iraq, the United States, along with a coalition of Allies liberated Kuwait. However,

Saddam Hussein, the leader in Iraq, remained in power and would remain a thorn in the side of this country.

It may be that George H W Bush will not go down in history as one of this country's greatest presidents, but he led the country very well. He was a president who was easy to admire and became even easier to admire after he left office. In the mind of this author, President Bush will always be thought of as an honorable man who longed for and strove to have a kinder and gentler nation and world.

In the election of 1992, the governor of Arkansas, William Jefferson Clinton, defeated President Bush. The defeat of Bush was probably somewhat attributable to the increase in taxes and the recession that had occurred in 1992. However, the primary reason for his defeat was due to the fact that H Ross Perot, a wealthy Texas businessman, ran as an independent and received more votes than any other third party candidate had ever received. Clinton won the election with forty-three percent of the popular vote.

President Clinton was the first president elected from the baby boom generation, which I have referred to as the Me Generation. Clinton grew up in humble surroundings in the state of Arkansas. He was a brilliant and articulate man. He governed from the political center. He was a master politician and governed without a strong set of predetermined principles, but maintained a keen sense of what the electorate wanted. In the early stages of his presidency, he proposed a large reform in the nation's health care system. It was defeated, and Clinton nimbly turned to other areas. He helped push through a tax increase, and it together with a vibrant economy, resulted in the first balanced budget in many years, and eventually in budget surpluses. He could also point to the lowest unemployment rates in modern times and a low inflation rate. During his term, the economy was aided by an increase in the productivity of American workers that in turn was assisted by technological advances.

In the 1996 election, Clinton defeated Robert Dole, a senator from Kansas who had also served as the leader of the Republicans in the Senate. In his first term, Clinton was supported by a Democratic majority in both the Senate and the House, but in the 1994 elections, both houses became controlled by the Republican Party. During his second term, the country continued to prosper. It may be that the technological advances of the 1990's deserved as much credit for the good economy as anything government did, but Clinton did everything that could be expected of government to aid the economy.

Despite his brilliance as a politician, President Clinton possessed a moral blind spot, as was unfortunately the case with too many of the people from the Me Generation. In 1996, Clinton became the second president to be impeached by the House of Representatives, but the Senate subsequently found him not guilty. His impeachment was the result of a number of indiscretions surrounding an affair with a young White House intern, Monica Lewinsky.

Clinton deserves the accolades he has received from many regarding his leadership during one of the most prosperous periods, if not the most prosperous period in the history of this country. However, he does not deserve high marks as a defender of faith-based morality. He demeaned the office of the presidency with the scandal that brought about his impeachment, and he held "pro-choice" views relating to abortion, which demean humanity. He made contributions to the prosperity of a nation, but fell short on pursuing a faith-based morality for this country.

As the twentieth century came to a close, it would be correct to call the United States a powerful country. After the end of the Cold War, this country became the lone superpower in the world. But, it did not regain its status as a great nation. More and more citizens began espousing a secular morality. Judges, and too frequently the Democratic Party, were siding with issues that can only be justified by secular viewpoints. Abortions continued at a high rate, the standing of the nuclear family was weakened as the long-held view that marriage should be solely between a man and a woman was being challenged. The merits of euthanasia were being advanced, and the death penalty remained a form of capital punishment. These ills eat at the fabric of society.

Other forms of secular morality too expanded. Drug use continued at a high rate. Movies and television were carriers of explicit sexual behavior, violence, and obscenities. Our youth were being exposed to such television and movies with little concern for the impact on them. The media had lost its standing as a defender of human rights and became advocates of "politically correct" issues. A once great nation was deviating more and more from the national code of morality intended by our founding fathers. When secular standards become a greater guide to the citizens and government officials of a nation, in effect there is no moral standard.

CHAPTER 16---THE START OF THE TWENTY-FIRST CENTURY

As our country prepared to enter a new millennium, we had entered the technological age. A major concern of this country and other countries was the ability of computers to transition properly from the year 1999 to 2000. With all the planning that went into that concern, it went off without a hitch.

In November of 2000, Albert Gore, vice president under Bill Clinton, was the Democratic Party nominee for president. George W Bush, governor of Texas, and son of the forty-first president of the United States, was the Republican nominee. It was an election that will long be remembered in the history of this country. In a close election, Gore won the popular vote and Bush won the Electoral College vote, but not in an uncontested manner.

The vote in Florida was extremely close, and its outcome would determine who would be the nation's forty-third president. The vote outcome favored Bush by a few hundred votes, but the Democrats challenged the results. After weeks of recounts and judicial proceedings, the Supreme Court, in a five-to-four vote, made the determination that Bush had won the vote in Florida, and thereby became president.

Eight months after taking office, Bush would face a challenge as great as any that had ever confronted this country. On September 11, 2001, terrorists struck this nation. On that day, terrorists hijacked four commercial airliners. Two were flown into the two World Trade Center towers in New York, and another was flown into the Pentagon in Washington, DC. The brave passengers of the fourth airliner decided to confront and assault the terrorists. The terrorists then decided to crash the plane in southwestern Pennsylvania, which may have saved many more of our citizens elsewhere. The exact destination of the fourth airliner remains unknown, but many believe the intended target was the White House or the Capitol.

The deaths from the crashes into the World Trade Center towers and the Pentagon exceeded 3,000, and it was a tragedy on the parallel of the attack on Pearl Harbor, sixty years earlier. After a number of wrenching days, President Bush promised the nation that all that could possibly be done, would be done, to bring the terrorists to justice. The chief perpetrator behind the attacks was Osama Bin Laden, a notorious terrorist, who was intent on imposing his fanatical view of the Islamic religion on the world. His view of Islam degrades the view of a fine religion, which as most religions, believes in a merciful and just Creator, and that people love one another. Extremists do not further the cause of religion.

It is hard to imagine that anyone's view of religion would include the killing of those who disagree with one's own warped views of a kind and merciful Creator. Bin Laden also wanted, and still wants, an end to the state of Israel and has vowed to harm anyone who, in any way, supports its existence.

Bin Laden's base of operations was in Afghanistan and his organization, al Qaida, was linked with the Taliban-headed government in that country. The Taliban also operated under the extreme Islamic brand of religion whereby they tortured and killed their own countrymen and women for little or no reasons. Because of their involvement with the terrorists who attacked this country, our government soon was at war in Afghanistan, and soon defeated the Taliban government. A new government was installed and is attempting to install a democratic government in that country.

The war that President Bush declared on terrorists is a new style of war. It is not waged by our country against any other specific country. But, because of

United States' superpower status, because of its defense of Israel as a nation, and because it is still the major defender of freedom in the world, it is a target of terrorists. The terrorists seek to destroy those who would hinder their imposition of a radical form of religion on the entire world. No religion that believes it has the right to torture and kill those who disagree with it has any right to claim it even remotely believes in a faith-based morality.

After the war in Afghanistan was over, this country was soon at war with Iraq, which was led by another fanatical man, Saddam Hussein, who had killed hundreds of thousands of people in his own country. President Bush took the country to war on the belief that Hussein posed a threat to people in his own region and the rest of the world by developing weapons of mass destruction, and by aiding and abetting terrorists. The war has become a political issue inasmuch as weapons of mass destruction in substantive amounts have not been found. The value of freedom to the long-oppressed Iraqi people has not been enough of a subject of the political debate. The unalienable rights of life, liberty, and the pursuit of happiness no longer seem to evoke the same sentiment in our citizens and politicians of today as they did to our founding fathers and those who fought for those rights over 200 years ago.

At this point in time, it is too early to assess the administration of George W Bush. He professes his belief of a faith-based morality and his position on matters involving major decisions bear out that belief. As this book was being written, President Bush was re-elected to a second term. President Bush has many of the qualities that have made great presidents. He has strong core values that are steeped in a faith-based morality. He believes strongly in freedom for people throughout the world and places the safety of this country's citizens at the top of his priorities.

However, it is impossible to view this country as a great country at this time, based on its adherence to a faith-based morality. Too many positions are being upheld and advanced that can only find their home in secularism.

Roe v. Wade continues to be the decision that permits abortions and the extinguishment of human life. Capital punishment, via the death penalty, is the law in most states. Both degrade humanity.

The marriage of gays and lesbians is being advanced and upheld by the judicial system in some areas of the country. That corrupts the intent of marriage between a man and woman that has been the norm since civilization began. It also devalues the concept of marriage and the nuclear family.

Sexual freedom for all, including our youth, is commonplace, as is obscenity and vulgarity in the media. They do not advance the general welfare of this nation. Sexual freedom is turning into an addiction among our youth.

Drugs and violence continue to run rampant in this country. It may be that their use is associated with the breakdown of the nuclear family. Members of the Me Generation, along with too many other Americans, have become too self-centered and no longer seem to care much about the freedom of others in this country, or in other countries. The focus on our personal status and power rarely serves the general welfare of a nation.

Too many judges and other political leaders blur the line that should be drawn between religion-based morality and faith-based morality. The First Amendment properly separated church and state. It did not separate faith and state, and unfortunately, too many judges and governmental leaders don't understand (or don't want to understand) the difference.

The media and government leaders are held in low esteem by a majority of our citizens, with good cause. The media now lacks independence, and government leaders are no longer statesmen. Power and self-preservation too frequently drive their agenda.

We are not, and have not been, a great country for the past forty years. We are still a superpower in the world, but as said at the outset of this book, power does not make a great country.

As long as a country devalues human life, promotes secular positions, takes selfish positions as citizens and as a country, and is not concerned about freedom, it cannot be called a great country.

Even though we may have too many bad traits to be a great nation, that does not mean we are a bad country. We have just lost some of our great traits, and hopefully, that is a short-term problem. We still rank high among all nations in the concerns for freedom of people around the world. It is just diminished from where it once was.

This is also an appropriate, and final, time to assess our country in relationship to the words of our good Scottish professor, Dr. Tyler. Let us first look at the beginning of the quote noted in the introduction of this book.

> *"A democracy cannot exist as a permanent form of government. It can only exist until the voters discover that they can vote themselves money from the public treasury. From that moment on, the majority always votes for the candidate promising the most money from the public treasury, with the result that a democracy always collapses over loose fiscal followed by a dictator."*

The above statement is debatable, but it has some elements of truth. We have become a nation that looks for too many handouts and promises from our government, with the result that our politicians promise more and more. The promises often go unfulfilled and when fulfilled, result in a larger national debt or higher taxes.

Those are the only significant sources of government income. The idea that we get things free from the government is a mirage.

We now have a Social Security system that is seriously underfunded and pays a poor rate of return to those who have contributed to the system. The same is true of Medicare.

The federal government involvement in education has only made our public education worse. It is a mirage to believe that a federal government can somehow improve education in all the large and small communities of the nation. Government's involvement in the educational process must be decentralized if it is going to be improved. The management concept of authority, responsibility, and accountability is essentially non-existent in our educational system. Do politicians discuss decentralization? No! Their answer is more and more spending, and more and more regulations. Spending and regulations from Washington D.C. do not, and will not, solve the problem in education.

In the 1960's, the federal government passed the Great Society legislation to eliminate poverty. Has poverty disappeared? No. Is it going to? Probably not. Now, the politicians continue to promise more to the poor, but don't count food stamps or other welfare benefits, that are already in place. Promises and more promises are the sign of the times.

The nation's federal debt is now between $7 and $8 trillion, and rising. That is more than $25,000 per every citizen of this country. We have truly mortgaged our children's future. The average family's share of the federal debt is now equivalent to a rather substantial home mortgage. Yet, the voters clamor for more and more benefits, which in turn will cost more and more, and that will mean higher taxes, or greater debt, or both. If the $9 to $11 trillion dollars of unfunded liability related to our Social Security system were included in the national debt figure, the per capita portion of such debt would approximate $60,000. We have reached a dangerous level of federal indebtedness.

Is it possible for a nation to reach the point that it can no longer sell its debt? Of course, it is. It has happened to a couple of South American countries in recent years and others have had to come to their financial aid. The politics of worrying about today, and getting elected, defers the consequences of the financial pothole this country is digging, and we just keep digging deeper.

Will the trend toward looking to the public trough continue? The answer based on history is not very hopeful.

Let us now look at the last part of Professor Tyler's statement.

"The average age of the world's great civilizations has been two hundred years. These nations have

> *progressed through the following sequence: from*
> *bondage to spiritual faith to great courage, from*
> *courage to liberty, from liberty to abundance,*
> *from abundance to selfishness, from selfishness to*
> *complacency, from complacency to apathy, from*
> *apathy to dependency, from dependency back to*
> *bondage."*

This country has exceeded the average of two hundred years. But, we enjoy a different freedom today than our forefathers did following the birth of this nation. Government entitlements now require a substantial part of the federal budget, whereas 200 years ago, that was not a function of the federal government. We have a monumental number of laws and regulations, which in turn require a monumental number of attorneys, and a monumental number of federal employees. The average taxpayer now pays between thirty and forty percent of his or her wages toward some type of local, state, or federal taxes. It may still be a democracy, or republic to some extent, but it would be more accurate to say it is a socialistic form of democratic government. Individual freedoms have been diminished because of the aforementioned situations, but the process has been gradual, and is accepted by most of the population, albeit they have only a moderate voice in the matter.

Spiritual faith, great courage, and liberty have been replaced with secularism in many areas, lack of fortitude in the defense of freedom, and an interest in personal power and affluence, instead of an interest in our follow humans.

We are still a land of abundance, although we have become a deeply and seriously indebted nation to ensure abundance, and we are most assuredly, a more selfish people than we have ever been. Complacency and apathy are real concerns. Many Americans no longer vote, and many no longer feel that their vote matters.

Dependency on government programs is now part of the American way. We have extensive welfare programs from the cradle to the grave. Citizens clamor for more with the belief that someone else is paying for the programs. "Don't tax thee, don't tax me, tax the person behind the tree" has become the hope of those who want more from government. The clamor to tax the rich increases, but that merely transfers capital needed to sustain economic growth to the government, which has little to do with economic growth.

Our government is no longer concerned with providing a free country, which permits citizens to succeed or fail, based on their willingness to work hard. It now feels it has a major role in determining how wealth should be taken from many and distributed to others.

We still rank among the best countries in this world. Are we as great a country as we once were? NO. We are drifting away from our spiritual faith and the faith-based morality of our forefathers. We have improved the lot of Black Americans, Native Americans, and women, but we are also devaluing humanity through abortions, euthanasia, and the death penalty, as well as the diminishment of the nuclear family. In the name of civil rights, we permit all types of degrading behavior, and effectively say general welfare does not matter. We have become more concerned with ME and less concerned with our neighbors.

Is Professor Tyler's evaluation correct? Despite all the expressions of concern I have noted in this book, it is still my opinion that events can and may take place which will give future generations a greater love of faith-based morality, a greater love of freedom, and a greater love of neighbor than the collective we of this country display today.

CHAPTER 17---GREAT LEADERS, GREAT MOMENTS AND THE FUTURE

During the course of doing research for this book, and in viewing our presidents from a slightly different perspective, I have altered slightly my views of our greatest presidents and will share my opinions with the readers of this book.

Number 1: Abraham Lincoln is my choice as our greatest president. In order to obtain freedom for slaves, he risked the breakup of our country, a bloody war, and his own life. He ignored the decision of the Supreme Court in the Dred Scott case. It was a courageous stand for the freedom of a race in this country. Slavery, which had been debated

143

from the birth of the country, was a stigma on the greatness of this country. Lincoln showed courage and determination in eliminating the worst stain on this country's greatness. He adhered as much as any president to the faith-based morality intended by the founding fathers. It should be noted that this was done despite the fact that Lincoln belonged to no specific religion.

Number 2: George Washington takes second place. He was the courageous and steady leader who led the country during the Revolutionary struggle and then led the country as its first president. He was admired in his own time and since. He was truly the father of our country.

Number 3: Franklin D. Roosevelt belongs in the third place of great presidents. He was the right man at the right time. He gave the country hope through the Great Depression and was never afraid to take action. He showed the same courage as he led the country during World War II. He did not let the crippling effects of polio deter him in his leadership of this nation through crisis after crisis.

Numbers 4 and 5: It is difficult to determine whether John Adams or Thomas   J e f f e r s o n deserve the fourth place as our greatest president, so I will call it a tie:

John Adams has been an underrated president, but no man sacrificed any more of his life than Adams did in serving his country. He laid the blueprint for our nation's Constitution with his work on the Massachusetts constitution. He opposed slavery from the beginning. He served ably in his many years of foreign service. He was a man of deeply held principles but thereby often provoked fellow politicians and his lack of willingness to compromise probably made him less a politician than many or most of our other presidents.

Thomas Jefferson ranks as one of our greatest presidents, not only for his leadership while president but also on the strength of the many things he did for this country before he was president. He was the initial drafter of the Declaration of Independence, one of this country's greatest documents that spell out the basic rights of human beings, which are endowed by our Creator.

It is always difficult to select the greatest presidents because we have had many that fall into the definition of great leaders. James Madison, Theodore Roosevelt, Woodrow Wilson, Harry Truman, and Ronald Reagan all fall into the category of great presidents.

This country has also had many periods of greatness. They are as difficult to rank as are the greatest presidents, but we will make an effort.

Number 1: The period of the late eighteenth century is, in my opinion, the greatest period of our country. The fight for freedom from England, the rights set forth in the Declaration of Independence, the adoption of our Constitution and the outstanding presidents in the early period of our country cannot be surpassed by any other great periods in our own country or in any other country.

Number 2: The period of the Civil War and the leadership of Abraham Lincoln run a close second as this nation's greatest period. After two hundred years of slavery, this country fought a fierce civil war to live up to the standard that this country believed all citizens were created equal, and had the right to life, liberty and pursuit of happiness.

Number 3: The period of 1932 to 1945 ranks as the third greatest period in this country's history, in my opinion. The actions of a great leader, Franklin D. Roosevelt, and the courage displayed by the citizens of this country during the Great Depression and World War II, must rank among the greatest of times in this country.

We have had other great periods of time, but the above three are times during which this country most closely adhered to a faith-based morality during difficult periods of our history. They were the times during which this nation indicated its great concerns for the freedom and liberty of all its citizens, and took the necessary action to ensure freedom. That attribute is one of the best indicators of a great nation.

Most historians tend to agree with the rankings of great leaders and great times because when we most closely adhere to the cause of freedom for all people, we generally tend to adhere most closely to a faith-based morality. We cannot always judge what is in the minds of people in regards to their love for their Creator, but we can see and judge the manner in which our leaders indicate their love of fellow human beings. Love of Creator and love of fellow humans are the primary ingredients of faith-based morality.

We have indicated that the last forty years of the twentieth century are not likely to be judged among the greatest periods in this country's history when viewed from an adherence to faith-based morality or from the concern of freedom for all people. It may be viewed as a period when the nation was the superpower of the world and enjoyed tremendous prosperity, but that alone, as noted throughout this book, is not enough to merit the definition of greatness.

We are a society that for the past forty years, has been excessively concerned with our personal welfare, and not concerned enough about the welfare of our fellow citizens in this country, or in other countries.

As long as we devalue the very existence of life through abortions, euthanasia, and the death penalty, we cannot wear the mantle of greatness.

As long as we devalue the status of a marriage between a man and woman and continue having a high percentage of divorces, we cannot wear the mantle of greatness. When we devalue the importance of a nuclear family, we devalue our youth and all of our citizens.

As long as we are a country that is addicted to the secular morality we find in drugs and sex, we cannot wear the mantle of greatness.

As long as we sell the idea of foul language, pornography, and other obscenities for profit or other motives, we cannot wear the mantle of greatness.

As long as we are excessively protective of our personal rights and freedoms, and care little about the rights and freedoms of all people in the world, we cannot wear the mantle of greatness.

The above failings all stem from a secular morality that implies humans have a better understanding of proper morality than those extended to us by a kind and loving Creator. As long as we as humans cling to that belief, we cannot and will not, correct the failings that deter from the label of a great country. We may still be among the best of countries, but we have slid downward from the lofty position we held after World War II.

During the 1920's we too were drifting toward being a country that seemed to value a certain amount of secular morality. The Great Depression and World War II gave us a better understanding that freedom and love for one another had to be at the top of a nation's priorities.

It is my view that some tragic event could swing this country back to a higher level of adherence to faith-based morality. When we understand better that our survival and our freedoms are at risk, we better appreciate our Creator.

It is also my view that there is hope in the higher level of faith-based interest that seems to be displayed by our youth. They seem to have a better appreciation of the gifts all of us receive daily from our Creator, our Supreme Being. Secular morality leaves a void in our lives. Such a void can only be satisfied by the understanding that someday, and in some manner, we will all answer to that Supreme Being. With that understanding, adherence to faith-based morality is made easier, and it is only with that understanding and our adherence to the wishes of a Supreme Being that our nation, and we as citizens, can be a great country and a great people.

About the Author

George E Pfautsch spent most of his working life as a financial executive for a major forests products and paper company. His final years at Potlatch Corporation were spent as the Senior Vice-President of Finance and Chief Financial Officer. His writings since retirement have little to do with finance. In an earlier book, "Redefining Morality - A Threat to our Nation", he examined the new moral standards of this country that are undermining the principles our founding fathers intended as a cornerstone to our Constitution. In this book, Pfautsch reviews the history of our nation and the role that the faith-based morality intended by our founding fathers played in the greatest periods of this country.

Printed in the United States
35434LVS00001B/157-408

9 781420 871890